Vinati Sukhdev started as a journalist, meandered into copywriting, foreign lands and strange territory, which included marriage and children. Currently, she heads Pratham UK—the fundraising arm of India's largest education NGO—which is a daily reminder that while we NRIs grapple with first-world problems like the ones described in the book, there are many other issues worthy of thought and action. The author's royalty from this book will go towards providing a better future to Pratham children.

East or West

AN NRI MOTHER'S MANUAL ON HOW TO BRING UP DESI CHILDREN OVERSEAS

Vinati Sukhdev

BGB

westland publications ltd
61, II Floor, Silverline Building, Alapakkam Main Road,
Maduravoyal, Chennai 600095
93, I Floor, Sham Lal Road, Daryaganj, New Delhi 110002

First published by westland publications ltd 2017

Co-published by westland publications ltd and
Bloody Good Book (www.bloodygoodbook.com)

10 9 8 7 6 5 4 3 2 1

ISBN: 978-93-86224-68-2

Designed by SÜRYA, New Delhi

Printed at Manipal Technologies Ltd, Manipal

For my parents who were born Indian
and my children who had Indianness thrust upon them.

I love you all.

CONTENTS

PREFACE

I did not plan to write this book. Nor did I plan to live outside India. But at some deep, subconscious level, I always wanted my children to be 'Indian'. At the start of my parenting journey, this was not an articulated desire. Like most new mothers, I was more concerned about naps and mealtimes. In fact, I had nothing to go on, except a deep love for the country where I was born and raised.

I loved India—deeply, unequivocally and even madly. As my Indian relatives never failed to point out, the fact that I did not live there made me love it even more over the years. Perhaps we non-resident Indians (NRIs) are nostalgic. Perhaps we fail to see the negative points of a large and still emerging country. Perhaps we do not have to deal with the drawbacks of living in India, such as power failure and corruption on a daily basis. Perhaps, all of the above.

It did not change the fact that I wanted to keep this love for India alive in my children. I had been a copywriter in advertising most of my working life and sold tyres and soap, tea and shampoo. How difficult could it be to sell India to my children? More difficult than I thought—but totally worth every fight and tantrum. Totally worth every hour I spent waiting outside Hindi and dance classes. Did I ever feel like giving up? Never!

Looking back, I do feel that a little bit of assurance would have helped. It was not easy in the early days and bringing up NRI children was an untouched subject. In fact, the more I think about it, the more amazed I am that no one has written such a book, despite the fact that there are millions of people out there who share the experience of raising children abroad. A recent estimate of Indians living outside India put the number at a staggering 25 million. A search on the internet revealed a bewilderingly broad suite of book titles in the parenting section: *Toddler—Spank or Not?*, *Eco-Baby—How to Rear a Baby the Eco-Friendly Way*, *Siblings Without Rivalry* and *The Step-Parents' Parachute*. There was even a book on how adopted children could find their parents on Facebook! But nothing, absolutely nothing on parenting Indian children abroad.

The second reason for writing this book was the hype surrounding two recent books: *Battle Hymn of the Tiger Mother* by Amy Chua and *How Opal Mehta Got Kissed, Got Wild and Got a Life* by Kaavya Viswanathan. Amy Chua's self-deprecating, witty novel about ethnicity-led strict parenting caused an uproar in liberal circles, while Kaavya's young adult novel about Asian parents trying to get their children into Ivy League schools created a small flutter before it was drowned out by allegations of plagiarism.

They made me think about my own parenting style and gave me the confidence to write on a subject I had no formal qualification for. I realised I was not Benjamin Spock nor Penelope Leach. Just a mum with over twenty years' experience and a fuzzy goal of bringing up 'Indian' children. But initial conversations with other NRI mums and the enthusiastic responses I got from them made me put my fingers on the keyboard. I realised I had something to say—something important; not because it was unique, but precisely because it was not unique. It was a shared experience that has not been articulated yet and, hopefully, sharing it formally in the form of a book, will lead to a more productive dialogue.

The third and final reason I decided to put myself out there (and it is not easy to share vignettes of private family life without feeling slightly foolish) is the strong belief that NRI children grow up confused if the Indian identity question is not addressed in some way by the parents. My belief was strengthened by the fact that I had observed older children of NRI friends going back to India in their late teens to 'discover' themselves.

I had observed, time and again, that NRI parents veer between two extremes—the strict 'no girlfriends/ boyfriends, no short dresses' variety and the too modern 'we are not really Indian, just ethnically different from the rest of the population'. According to me, being different ethnically does create a dissonance in the child's identity and this issue needs to be explored and addressed in the parenting years—in a balanced way—which I found largely missing.

Finally, the idea of this book is to start a dialogue on this subject rather than prescribe rules. What makes my book different from other parenting manuals is that it does not set out to be the best way or the only way to bring up children abroad. It is unapologetically Indian—by an Indian and for Indians—though other ethnic minorities, particularly from Asia, will be able to identify with many of the issues. I can only describe 'my way' and since I have produced two children who most people describe as balanced and well brought-up, it is one possible way. That's all.

Hope you enjoy your parenting journey as much as I did.

I

INTRODUCTION

We Are Like This Only!

What makes us 'Indian'? And what aspects of 'Being Indian' should we distil for our children?

Competition! Visa issues! Part of big crowds. *Jugaad.*

Nuclear plus Parents. **Family is everything!**

Tricolour. Our tolerant attitude. **Belief in non-violence.** Respect for elders and guests (including foreigners).

Excellence in fields like medicine and mathematics.

Belief in the karma theory/rebirth. **Conflict.** Complicated relationships!

Chalta hai. **Resilience.** Tradition. **Family values and strong ties.** ***Athithi Devo Bhava.***

Willingness to accept corrupt/useless/moronic politicians as leaders. Unity in diversity.

Vasudhaiva kutumbakam! Comfort with contrasting ideas. Hard work. **Kismat.**

Grandparents. Aunts. ***Chaat.*** Home food. **Smell of *bela* (jasmine).** Dirty public toilets. **Train journeys.** Ayahs, cooks, drivers. **Bucket baths.**

Swalpa adjust madi (Kannada)—*jara adjust kar lena* (Hindi) or *thoduh adjusting hwave* (Marathi)….Hence the eight people in a car meant for four, ten guests when there are four beds!

Food—we even carry our cooks around with us all over the world.

Noise—we speak loudly no matter where we are.

Cinema—we love our movies and our movie stars.

Poppadoms. **Home-made pickles, and such food items.** Emotional.

Compulsive matchmaking—*Iska ladka uski ladki!* Warmth.

Open arms—*apnapan*. Big fat weddings. **Jewellery.** *Saas-bahu.*

Bhai-bhatijawad. Bribes. **Family.** Values. **Faith.** Respect for elders.

▸•◂

All these comments are actual replies to an email I sent out to NRI friends and family asking what being Indian means to them—in one word or sentence.

I do not dare define being Indian, for the purposes of this book or anything else for that matter. It is a country of over a billion people. A democracy, where there are a billion views on what being Indian means. So I guess I took the easier way out—I left it to others. Mainly my NRI friends and family. And the answers were very interesting indeed!

There were the expected themes of family, family values, respect for elders and tradition, which cropped up again and again. But there were also newer entrants—media-led words like 'jugaad' which the world now acknowledges as a uniquely Indian gift to the world. It means the frugal innovation that is now being attempted in large international corporates in a world that recognises natural resources are limited and the economy still fragile.

There were positive and negative spins on the same theme of what being Indian means. Some of my friends and family called the Indian capacity to absorb foreign influences 'tolerance' and 'unity in diversity', while others defined it as '*chalta hai*' or 'anything goes'. Yet others condemned the Indian habit of suffering corrupt politicians silently. Definitely, two sides to the same coin.

For instance, Indians do seem to adhere to the 'kindly adjust' theme in every way—good and bad. So there will be eight people in a five-person car and lots of warmth and sharing but also apathy to dirt in public areas and corrupt politicians. Some said Indians were loud, others thought they were warm and friendly. Again, perhaps, two sides of the same coin.

Food was an unexpected contender for the top spot in the replies—such was the enthusiasm to define what

'Indian' was. Even specifics like pickles, chaat and papad were mentioned! *Athithi Devo Bhavah* ('Guest is God') and *Vasudhaiva kutumbakam* ('The world is my family') got a look-in, but it was family and food all the way! Gulab jamuns scored over the *grihastha* ashram and kababs over karma!

So, if distilled for parenting, what does 'Being Indian' actually mean? A few key values emerge and these are discussed in the pages that follow. They are:

Art, History and Culture: India is an ancient civilisation and knowledge of and pride in the culture can only be an asset.

Language: It is important that children know at least one Indian language. It paves the way for ease and familiarity with the environment on trips to India, and serves as an important link to the culture.

Academics and Careers: The Indian values of hard work and thrift in order to succeed are characteristic of most Indian families. At an event held at Wembley Stadium on the occasion of Prime Minister Narendra Modi's visit to the UK, British Prime Minister David Cameron spoke glowingly about the British Indian community who, he said, had put the 'Great' in Great Britain. He added that the UK had a lot to learn from their values of hard work, enterprise and family relationships. Surely, we don't need a non-Indian to tell us that! Make sure your children hear this from you and imbibe it.

Marriage: You don't have to force your children into arranged marriages, but it is important to teach them why the Indian values of tolerance and 'kindly adjust' help make all relationships work better—including marriage. A little less 'I' and a little more 'we' is a recipe for a happier life. Indians sometimes do not take kindly to their children marrying foreigners and I have discussed the possible reasons for this.

Family Relationships: The importance of a harmonious, stable family life cannot be emphasised enough. As broken homes and single parents become more common in the West, Indian children growing up in relatively stable environments have a lot to be thankful for. The parenting of Indian children continues well into their adult years, sometimes with comical results, but by and large most Indian children, young and old, love and appreciate their selfless parents.

Though I did not put pen to paper for twenty-seven years while I 'parented', subconsciously I was doing what I had set out to do and what I would urge my readers to do. I distilled what I thought was positive and valuable about being Indian and I created a bridge to Indian culture and values.

I made sure my kids learnt an Indian language. I gave them exposure to Indian art, history and culture so they could embrace the Indian side of their global identity and take pride in it. I stressed that the family was important to Indians, even the extended family; marriage meant marrying a family not a person, and so on. I made sure they worked hard at their academics and prepared for careers. I was playing by my own rules, imprinting the chapters of this book on my children's minds without even realising it. They responded positively as well.

When it was time to choose a foreign language as part of their university curriculum, both of them unhesitatingly opted for Hindi. They welcomed all holidays to India even though it meant meeting grandparents and cousins again and again—and yet again! They experimented with Indian clothes and looked forward to Diwali and Holi every year. They learnt Indian dance and music. But, more importantly, they learnt to love the Indian side of their global identity and take pride in it.

It was not always easy. Along the way, there was a lot of learning and unlearning to do—for both my children and for me. I had to understand that they would never be exactly like me—for instance, they would never have the kind of in-depth knowledge of the various kinds of Indian communities that I have. They are still surprised at how I can say that a person is a Pahadi Brahmin when I encounter a Pant or Pande and almost always be right. Or guess that someone is a Jat Sikh because the surname is Mann or Brar. These are the kind of things that one learns from living in India all one's early life and going to school with the Joshis and Manns. On the other hand, they do not get their Vs and Ws mixed up as I still do, almost twenty-five years after leaving India, and that is surely a good thing!

Similarly, there are obviously some traits like being

chronically late (or on Indian Standard Time), which you do not want to instil in your children! However the knowledge of a cyclical rather than linear view of time can be useful in a globalising world where your child might actually be working in India one day. Similarly, food is an important tool to draw children into Indian culture and heritage. Maybe food journeys across India would be the answer.

The important thing is that my girls are learning all the time and, more importantly, are keen to learn more about India. And they do know enough about Indian names and texts to realise that Kabir is both a Hindu and Muslim name and that is why Vikram Seth chose it for a character in *A Suitable Boy* as a way of keeping his religious identity a bit of mystery. And that is a triumph for me.

So you have to make sure that the picture of India that you present to your children is interesting and colourful and keeps the door to their mother country open. Your children, being naturally curious and adventurous, will walk through it and embrace what they like. Part of being Indian is diversity, so it may be different aspects of India for different children. It could be wildlife and forest sanctuaries for one family; it could be mountain trekking for another and *dadi's sarson ka saag* for yet another—but the sights, sounds and familial warmth will enrich their lives and yours, I promise you that.

It would not be fair if I do not spell out a few notes of caution for parents about to embark on this important journey. Remember, your children live in a foreign eco-system. There is a lot of peer pressure to contend with along the way. How do you stress the importance of family relationships when hanging out with grandparents or even parents is not 'cool' amongst a lot of Western teenagers. I considered this a significant point of difference and made it clear to my children that 'we' were different and that grandparents and relatives like *maasi*s and *chacha*s were important to us.

There was a bit of rebellion along the way. When she was thirteen, my daughter Ashima once refused to walk down Singapore's main street with her visiting grandparents, in case she was spotted by her classmates, and I remember being shocked and angry. However, I had the sense to realise it was a passing phase. I made my displeasure clear and once she saw her sister getting all the attention from the grandparents, Ashima was quick to mend her ways. Ultimately, *laad-pyaar* and *nani's besan laddoos* triumphed!

Thanks to the importance given to familial relationships in the early years, I am proud to say that my parents and my children have a deep and loving relationship today. My parents spent last summer living with their two adult granddaughters in New York. Before they arrived, Ashima happily 'granny-proofed' the flat and Mahima applied face paint in Argentinian flag colours on her *nana's* forehead as they watched the football World Cup final at a sports bar in NYC. Now that is Indian family life at its best. It is worth striving for—even in the difficult and rebellious years in between.

SUMMARY

The concept of what makes us Indian is hard to define—but certain values are easy to spot: meaningful family relationships, hard work leading to material success, being tolerant of others and being spiritual are examples.

Distilled for parenting, 'Being Indian' means taking all these positive values and making sure children growing up in a foreign eco-system are exposed to them.

It is not an easy journey—children rebel at what they consider 'foreign' and 'strange' requests or demands from parents. Peer pressure makes them conform to the peer group rather than be perceived as different.

Recognise that your children will never be as 'Indian' as you, and appreciate every baby step they take towards discovering India.

Enjoy the journey—it is worth it!

2

WHERE ARE YOU FROM?

Simple Question...Complex Answer

'Where are you from?' Pause. Like most 'third culture kids' brought up outside the country of their birth and passport, I had always been that bit slower to respond. There had never been a right answer. The person could be asking for my current address, in which case a sentimental journey to India, the land of my birth, would be pointless. Or it could be a deeper question about identity or culture, and saying 'near London NW8' would not quite answer it. For many angst-ridden years, I continued to grapple with the right answer.

Until I met Ramu.

It was the evening rush hour in Mumbai—a city of 18 million that pours its office-workers from downtown towards the northern suburbs in a slowly coagulating stream of traffic along a single arterial route. Ramu was an enterprising ten-year-old selling the evening tabloid at a crowded traffic junction. He had mastered the art of wending his reed-thin body between cars, thrusting the paper into the ones that had their windows open and knocking urgently on the air-conditioned ones to attract attention. He knew precisely how many minutes it would take to collect loose change from the customers who had been sufficiently enticed by his aggressive marketing of the day's sensational story. Today seemed a particularly good day. India had just won a thrilling cricket match against Australia and while everyone had seen the match earlier (Indian offices are notorious for coming to a complete halt during cricket matches), it was now time to look at the statistics, revel in the description of the enemy being felled and see evidence of the victory in print.

As we slowly crept up to the head of the queue, it was our turn. Ramu hurried to us with his victory celebration routine in full swing. 'Rahul Dravid ne *Australia* ko haraya,*' he shouted lustily. This could be loosely translated as 'Rahul Dravid conquers Australia,' but then cricket in India is seen as just that—an epic battle on which national pride and honour are staked. His dirt-streaked face, unremarkable in other aspects, was alight with joy. 'Sister, don't you want to read this good news about your country?' he urged. I was fumbling in my bag for the right change and realised I had none. He, salesman par excellence, did not need to be told. 'No matter, sister, it is good news for India and I want to share it with you—pay me tomorrow.' And he was gone.*

My reply, 'But I don't live here' and 'I will never come back', got stuck in my throat—along with a big lump that is still there when I think of him. I have to now confess I don't know his name, but I have given him one because, for me, he and all others like him will never be statistics of poverty any more. They are people like you and me who have the capacity to dream, share and give.

I realised that in all my years of confused searching, I had been caught up in an unseeing middle-class huddle of, 'Yes, I was born in India but have escaped it.' Or a smug karmic 'Yes, I was born in a poor country but thankfully not on the streets.' Most people living in India practise a 'no eye-contact with poverty' survival technique that I was not familiar with. I had done the unthinkable. I had let a strange child into my conscience and heart. And I am so glad I did. I went back to Singapore and joined the Bombay Street Kids charity run at my school, working tirelessly and happily for two years. I have made community work my priority in my current school in the UK. And, most important of all, I am involved with other people and not searching for who I am. Ramu decided that for me...I was an Indian girl who was as keen on cricket as he was.

And yes, thank you, Ramu. I need to say that, because I forgot to say it that day.

—Mahima writing on the identity question
that had vexed her teenage years

▸•◂

Our daughter Mahima may have been unique in the way she chose a kindred spirit at a traffic light to solve her identity issue, but she is certainly not alone. Estimates suggest that over 220 million people now live in countries not their own ethnically—making them comprise the fifth largest nation on earth! So there are a lot of possible answers to the question: 'Where are you from?'—and for Indian children and parents living abroad, a multitude of ways to decide how little or how much they want India to shape their identity.

Broadly speaking, parenting abroad is what my husband and I called the 'Roots vs Wings' debate. Added to the usual dynamics of living in a culture that is non-Indian, we had our own differences about how Indian we felt and how much we wanted India to shape our children. Pavan left India when he was thirteen and went to schools in Switzerland and England before graduating from the University of Oxford. He absorbed Western culture and music while he was at boarding school along with the English mush that passed for food. He listened to Mahler when he was sad and celebrated happy occasions with champagne. His academic discipline at university was astrophysics, which was about universal principles, there being nothing Indian about dark holes or light or matter. He did, however, head the India Society at Oxford, but again his relationship with India was what most Indians would consider very 'foreign'. He appreciated Indian classical music and invited Hari Prasad Chaurasia and other classical musicians to perform at his Society meetings. He got Indian academicians to voice their opinions on the Shah Bano case in his intellectual university magazine. He had not seen a single Bollywood film till I dragged him to one, but he had a Sanskrit tutor teach him the language during vacations in India. He is like the Beatles, I remember telling an Indian friend during our early courtship days—he knows and loves a part of India that most of us don't know or have forgotten!

I, on the other hand, grew up in India, solidly and steadfastly, and lived there happily until I absolutely had to leave because of my husband's job. I thought happy occasions meant *laddoo*s and *halwa* and cried when I heard Lata Mangeshkar sing '*Ae Mere Watan ke Logon*'. I went to book fairs at Pragati Maidan in Delhi and read Russian novels thrust on the captive Indian market by the USSR, as it was known in those days. I thought Westernisation and material success were evil and my long essay topic in my final year of college was 'Multinational Corporations and the Havoc they Wreaked on the Economy'. Did we have different sensibilities? Absolutely. Different temperaments? Not a doubt. He was a third culture kid living outside the country of his birth and passport. I was an Indian girl growing up in pre-liberalised India. Yet we fell in love with each other's differences and got married.

So when it came to the children, there were obviously very divergent views. I wanted them to be 'rooted' in India emotionally, spiritually and culturally, if not physically. Pavan wanted to give them wings—the best possible education in the world, a global perspective, a worldview that would first encompass the whole world and then change it! According to him, it was not about where they were from but where they were going. I felt they needed to have a 'home' before they travelled. According to me, if you looked a certain way, that is, non-white, there would always be a chasm in that identity unless it was filled with the language and culture of your racial origin.

I had met numerous ABCDs (American Born Confused Desis) and BBCDs (British Born Confused Desis) who did not know an Indian language, spoke English just like Americans and British white people do and indeed, thought they were American or British: 'Hi, I'm Drove (Dhruv) from Milwaaaakee,' or 'Hey, I'm Jas (Jasminder) from Birmingham.' I knew we lived in a rapidly globalising world but I was not so sure race and identity questions could be swept away so lightly.

I had an Indian friend in the US who had named her son Michael, drove him to soccer and took photos of him dressed in his first tuxedo at his high school prom. He was as American as apple pie. Imagine her surprise then when, just after graduating from High School, he announced that he wanted to live in Mumbai for a year and learn Hindi. She was wise enough to let him do it. But I did not want any surprises when the girls were eighteen. I was going to make an effort to fill their identity vessel with the 'India' I knew.

Very early on and in the interest of family harmony, my husband and I decided we would both impart to them what we knew best and loved. There was a great deal of compromise and give and take along the way. There were a few bumps too. But on the whole, it was a fulfilling journey and we both thought the girls got the best out of us. We also understood that the girls would turn out to be an amalgam of what we gave them—neither totally Indian, nor totally global. They would be different from other children and even different from each other.

So, in our family, the father organised trips to nature parks and wildlife trails, while the mother scouted for Indian dance classes. The father was the guiding light on 'cosmopolitan' subjects like science and maths, while the mother gave ideas for creative writing (always about India); the father spoke French and helped with French homework, the mother took them to Diwali fairs and explained that the festival of lights was five days long. The father brought back teddy bears from the various hotels he stayed at, while the mother brought back *Panchatantra* comics and *Mahabharat* DVDs from various trips to India. In the car, the father played classical FM while the mother kept an old calendar sheet with the family tree drawn behind it so that the children would use long car journeys to learn which cousin belonged to what side of the family. Both agreed to speak to the children in Hindi for the first few years of their lives (we were lucky in this regard, for we shared a common language). Both agreed that being a good person and making the best use of your abilities and education was a great starting point in life. And so our children grew up—both Indian and not Indian.

From very early on, they knew which parent to turn

to and for what. While Mahima's searching essay on her Indian identity may suggest confusion, this was a confusion that was confined to the 'mother' space in her life. If you consider her dilemma carefully, she was searching for a way to define her Indian side. Her reaction to the boy was not Indian in any way, but a conscionable way to react to the extreme poverty she saw. She says she did the 'unthinkable' by establishing eye contact with poverty. She certainly did not want to be Indian in the sense that Indians living in cities often are—unseeing and uncaring. She wanted to be a global Indian—someone who actually gave the boy a name, elevated him to the level of a kindred spirit. She says she went back to her school's community service programme with a renewed determination to help boys like him. So the dilemma was not whether she was Indian or not (her mother had made sure being Indian would always be a part of her identity), it was a question of defining and shaping that identity so it would merge into a broader global identity nurtured by her father and not be at odds with it. She had done what all children do—she merged various influences from both parents seamlessly and in her own unique way.

So the first step—whether you like it or not—is to understand that your children are not going to turn out to be like you. Even if both of you are from an almost identical background in India, your children will not be the same. They have an identity that is uniquely their own. As parents, we seek to influence that identity and shape it, but it never truly belongs to us. Our children will always be a little 'less' Indian than us—in the way they speak, in the way they think. But they might also turn out to be 'more' Indian than us. Pavan's parents, while fluent in Hindi, certainly did not know Sanskrit; their son's interest in a classical Indian language made him 'more' Indian than they were. You might have strummed a guitar during your youth, but your son (born and brought up outside India) might display an interest in the tabla. Does that make him 'more' Indian or 'less' Indian than you? These are all subtle gradations of identity along a sliding scale and, in today's rapidly globalising world, who's to say who's Indian and how Indian!

Having said that, the Indian diaspora is unique in its single-minded pursuit of preserving an Indian identity through language, culture and food. Compare the Caribbean community in the UK with the Indians who came via Africa. The Caribbeans arrived in the '50s; today, some sixty years later, they have almost no links with their mother country, have adapted British customs and manners, and are proud to be black and British. The Gujaratis came in the '70s, displaced from Uganda by Idi Amin. They had left India even earlier, hundreds of years ago, sailing from Gujarat to Africa to find a better life. Yet they speak Gujarati fluently, and so do their children. In fact, my Gujarati friends from Mumbai claim they cannot understand British Gujarati because it is an old-fashioned version that is hardly used in India today. When India won the Cricket World Cup in Calcutta in 2011, predominantly Gujarati areas, like Wembley in

London, erupted in a blaze of fireworks and celebrations. There were huge crowds outside on the streets, the traffic totally disrupted by pedestrian mobs who had taken over the roads, waving the Indian flag, shouting *Jai Hind.* I remember going to see the celebrations at Kingsbury that night and thinking, 'My goodness, how proud these young people are to be identified with India!'

A corollary to that, of course, is how tenuous that link is. The Indian High Commission in London routinely turns down applications from these 'Indians' wanting the coveted badge of honour—the Overseas Citizen of India passport. They cannot prove they have a link with India because their forefathers left the country before birth certificates were issued as a procedure. As a result, they can never hope to establish a formal link between their Indian ethnicity and their 'mother' country. Yet in their hearts and minds, they feel 'Indian'. And that is testimony to the way the Indian identity has been preserved by their parents—across continents and through centuries.

So the African Gujaratis, the Singapore Tamilians, the Californian Sikhs (all of whom migrated from India several generations ago), have all shown us it can be done. The Indian identity *can* be preserved and passed down to our children successfully. Provided we NRI parents realise that our children will never be exactly like us, this is an enterprise worth embarking on.

As parents we are responsible for shaping our children's attitudes towards India and Indians, helping them build their own global Indian identity that, though not exactly like our own (if we have grown-up entirely in India), is an identity they cherish and are proud of. I do not mean proud in a jingoistic, nationalist way but as part of an ethnic heritage they understand, are knowledgeable about and are, therefore, happy to embrace.

Over the years, I have seen too many instances of an Indian identity being foisted on reluctant NRI children by parents who do not distil the essence of India, just the outer trappings. 'No, you cannot do that, Indian girls do NOT go to the pub,' or 'No, you cannot have a white girlfriend.' Naturally, the children resent it. As intelligent, aware beings with access to the internet, they soon realise, for example, that there are pubs and bars and clubs sprouting up all over modern India and wonder why their parents refuse to move with the times. This fuels their resentment and anger. Instead of just a generation gap, they have to struggle with a time lag too. Their parents seem frozen in the India they left twenty or thirty or even hundreds of years ago. Many of these children decide to segregate the two aspects of their personality. They are cosmopolitan with their friends (often secretly clubbing, dating, drinking and smoking) while being 'Indian' at home. This is not a happy situation. It can only tear families apart as parents discover what has been going on behind their back and the children are wracked by guilt. It leads, in extreme cases, to forced marriages and even suicides.

This unhappy, double life does not bring fulfilment to the children either. They are torn between two very different worlds, ashamed and inferior about being 'different' from their mates and far from proud or fulfilled in their Indian identity. Meera Syal, actress and author and an evocative spokesperson for the British Indian community, describes the angst of just such a girl in her novel *Anita and Me*. Set in a working class neighbourhood in an East Midlands village in the '70s, the 'Me' of the title is a twelve-year-old Indian girl called Meena who is taken up with the glamorous Anita Rutter, a long-legged blonde girl who lives in the house next door but who could be living in a world apart from Meena. For Meena, the confusion of adolescence is compounded by the fact of being 'different' from everyone else in the neighbourhood. She squirms every time a relative arrives to pinch her cheeks, cringes when her parents speak their accented English and longs to be like Anita, the Westernised, *Jackie* magazine-reading, flirtatious teenager that Meena was never allowed to become by her Indian parents. By shoring up their defences against Western culture at a vulnerable time in the early immigrant experience, Indians like Meena's parents were behaving true to type. They were protecting their identity in harsh circumstances amidst racist and often hostile neighbours. Why this attitude should persist forty years later cannot be explained—or forgiven.

Far from bringing up 'Indian' children, this sort of parenting only results in duplicitous behaviour and children who equate India with inflexible traditions. Anyone familiar with India knows that this is not the case. India's triumph has been acceptance and absorption. In the long sweep of history, 'foreigners' have invaded India from the north and along its coastlines, only to be absorbed and converted to the Indian way of life. So this unbending attitude is certainly not 'Indian' or very useful, as it turns out.

Then there are other NRI parents, certainly amongst more recent immigrants, who go to the other extreme. They eschew anything remotely Indian. *Desi* equals inferior, even bad, in their new lives. Why eat *parathas* when you can eat pasta? Why mess with Hindi when you can learn Spanish? The children are sent to ballet classes and made to practise the piano. When asked where he is from, little Nick (Nikhil actually, but Nick is so much easier) has no hesitation at all in saying 'I am from Greenwich, Connecticut.' Holidays to India for these children consist of duty-bound visits to grandparents whom they can neither relate to, nor feel any real affection for. Lack of an Indian language hampers interaction and makes the whole experience stressful and tiresome. I even know someone who has an American wife and feels he cannot subject his children or his wife to his parents' middle-class home in India. So they check into a five-star hotel and make sporadic and sweaty forays to the trans-Yamuna colony in East Delhi where his parents live. 'My father is so unbending,' he confided recently, 'he will just not let me upgrade his home. I was willing to do it all at my expense.' When last heard of, even the occasional visits to the grandparents' home had been stopped. They lived in an adjoining suite at the hotel instead!

I feel sorry for the children in these families, who will grow up thinking of India as a dangerous place where they could fall ill or get kidnapped. They will absorb the view of the father who is clearly diffident about, if not ashamed, of his country of origin. They will never know or enjoy the wonderful spontaneity of childhood—the cuddles from the grandparents, the pinching of cheeks by total strangers, making new friends in the park, learning about different kinds of mangoes and discovering the delights of jalebis and *gulab jamun*s. My children have spent many a happy (and sweaty) summer in India doing all this and more. Children are not judgmental—they are free spirits who cannot tell a municipal park in India from their posh Tumble Tots gym in the US, UK or Hong Kong. They want to have fun, they want to learn and absorb new experiences and as parents, we have to make sure they are allowed to do so. Early childhood memories will shape their Indian identity. If they've had fun with friends and family during holidays to India, they will always enjoy different aspects of the country. I am certainly not advocating recklessness, such as letting the children eat street food in India (they may fall ill), but surely there is a medium between that and keeping them cosseted in a bubble that never allows them to experience India.

Having realised fairly early that childhood influences would shape my children's reaction to India, I started making some conscious choices. Instead of just the grandparents' home, our holidays to India began to take in wildlife parks and heritage sites. My parents would gamely accompany us (they were relatively young in those days) so the family bonding was not disrupted. On these trips, Mahima and Ashima not only experienced the delights of municipal parks in Delhi but also the Church of Francis of Assisi and the Mangeshi temple in Goa, the Taj Mahal and the Bharatpur bird sanctuary. We never quite managed it—but I would recommend the Buddhist trail which takes in Nalanda and Sarnath and the Ajanta and Ellora caves in Maharashtra. India has so much to offer outside the crowded cities, it is a pity that more NRI parents don't take advantage of rapidly improving tourist facilities and communications. The Indian Railways are another great way to explore India. I know a family that bought a one-month pass and chugged along the length and breadth of India. Their son recalls the magic of going to sleep in central India one night with the vendors outside on the platform shouting *chai, chai garam garam chai* (hot tea for sale) and waking up to the smell of coffee and cries of *kaffee, kaffee, kaffee* as the train crawled into south India when dawn was breaking. These little facts—that north Indians drink tea and south Indians are predominantly coffee drinkers (including bed coffee) were not important in themselves, but they helped him establish a connection with India—his personal geography of an India defined by beverages.

By helping your children carve out their own definition and vision of India, you will help it become an indelible part of their identity. Travel across India is a good way to do this in an interesting and engaging way, although undertaking it is not easy. It takes persistence and planning and effort. It takes standing up to relatives asking, 'Why are you dragging such little children all over India?' It takes sacrifices—we never went to Legoland in Denmark, for instance (school holidays are always limited and India so vast), but most of all, it takes believing in yourself and loving India. And with that, I had no problem!

Travel is just one of the many ways that will shape your child's Indian side—it is conversations at the dining table, it is remarks that you don't even know the children are listening to, it is the books they see lying around the house, it is the art and the music that surrounds them. Children are like sponges that will absorb everything. Show me a child who loves reading Indian authors writing in English and I will show you their parents' library stacked with Salman Rushdie, Vikram Seth and Amitav Ghosh. Point out an NRI child knowledgeable about Indian music and I can bet one of the parents is interested in it. So make sure your children have an Indian environment at home—and that does not necessarily mean Indian objects. It could be the emphasis on family relationships, it could be a philosophy of spirituality and acceptance or it could be an ethic of hard work. You will be surprised to see how much your children pick up your 'Indian' way of life.

Your children's identity is, ultimately, as unique as their biometrics—an amalgam of all the influences that have shaped them—including their parents, their journeys, their education, their environment and their various homes in different parts of the world. I have an Indian cousin who calls Boston (where he lives) his bedroom, New York his living room, Los Angeles (where he owns a home) his garden and Dusseldorf (where his Indian parents now live) his kitchen. He is single, travels to see his parents once a month and considers himself Kashmiri, Indian, German, American—all at the same time. He grew up in Mumbai but moved to Germany with his parents at the age of sixteen. Germany is 'home' he said to me once, and Mumbai is 'home-home'. He is completely global today, but Indian enough to fly all the way to New York and take his cousin (me) and niece out to dinner. New York is, after all, his living room and as for most Indians, the family comes first!

In today's rapidly globalising world, there are an increasing number of people who consider more than one place home and your children will probably fall into that category. Travel writer and essayist Pico Iyer who was born in Britain, but has lived in the US and Japan, besides travelling extensively, spoke evocatively on the subject in his 2013 TED talk. According to Iyer, 'Home is not where you happen to be born, it is where you become yourself.' He himself has been shaped by his Indian ethnicity, his education in the US and his love for Japan. Home has 'less to do with soil and more to do with soul,' he says. I couldn't agree more. As parents we have to distil the soul of India and implant it in our children. We must make them proud of their Indian heritage as part of their global identity. That is the best gift we can give them.

SUMMARY

In today's globalising world, the identity issue is an increasingly important one: not confined to you and your children. It is estimated that 220 million people now live in countries that are not their own ethnically.

It is possible for both parents to have different views of how Indian they want their children to be. Each parent should impart to the children the aspect of India that they know best and love most.

The Indian diaspora is unique in its ability to preserve the Indian identity and we should be proud of that.

Old-fashioned immigrant parents caught in a time warp, who foist an Indian identity on their children, are doing the wrong thing: Indian parenting is not about being strict or inflexible.

Parents who go to the other extreme and keep their children away from India, and all things Indian, are depriving their children of an authentic and spontaneous experience of their mother country and leave a gaping hole in their children's identity kit.

The answer is to be judicious and balanced. Parents are key influencers—remember your children will turn out to be an amalgam of all their experiences. Make them proud of their Indian heritage as part of their global identity.

3

MUM AND DAD OR AMMA AND BABA

Early Parenting—The Dilemmas Begin Earlier Than You Think!

Day 1: Your bedtime tale is about the moon who is a favourite uncle and a great cook.

Chanda mama door ke, pooey pakaein boor ke
Aap khayen thali mein, munne ko de pyali mein

Day 2: You switch to another language and a different nursery rhyme. Now the moon is part of an obstacle course for a cow.

Hey diddle diddle, the cat and the fiddle
The cow jumped over the moon
The little dog laughed to see such sport
And the dish ran away with the spoon

Day 3: It is time to be an Indian parent again. Your little baby hears you talk about the fish who is queen of the ocean, never to be hunted.

Machchli jal ki rani hai
Jeevan uska pani hai
Haath lagao dar jayegi
Bahar nikalo mar jayegi

Day 4: You sing a different tune in a different language. The fish is being hunted and it has to bite in order to survive, ouch!

One two three four five
Once I caught a fish alive
Six seven eight nine ten
Then I let it go again
Why did you let it go?
Because it bit my finger so!

—The dilemma of multi-lingual parents
as narrated by a first-time mother

▸•◂

How different can babies be? All they seem to need in the early years is nourishment and love. Surely these needs are universal? What is so Indian about sleep times or lactating or mushy food? How many different ways can there be to cuddle a child?

Yes, at a certain level, all babies are the same, but the way love and nourishment are provided can be dictated by culture. NRI parents are often caught in the trap of bringing up Indian babies abroad with very little help, hugely conflicting advice from different sources and cultural asks that seem difficult, if not impossible. This makes an already stressful time even more fraught.

'Nobody prepared me for how difficult it was going

to be,' says an ex-Goldman Sachs banker. From being an efficient woman who was totally in-charge of her personal and professional life, she recalls how she was reduced to feeling inept and hopeless because she kept competing with her counterparts in India and felt the cultural tug of war just did not help because she did not have the same family support or domestic help. 'I was not in a position to say, "Okay, *beta*, you don't like *bhindi* so I am going to make you some *aloo* instead."'

Another successful professional recounts that she felt hopeless and blamed herself for absolutely everything that went wrong. If the baby had colic, it was her fault. If the baby was underweight, she was a bad mother. And when her baby refused to latch on to her breast she felt positively sub-human. She remembers the first five months of her baby's life as a complete nightmare, with her pumping her breast milk into a bottle and getting her son to feed. It took her visiting Indian mother-in-law to throw away the pump. 'Stop being a cow and start being a mother,' was her sage advice—born of common sense which is neither Indian nor Western. Looking back on the incident, the young mum says, 'I think the difference is that a Western mother-in-law would not have interfered. While Western parents and in-laws help from time to time, it is all within boundaries and they would never dare interfere, let alone throw away a breast pump. But that is just what I needed and I am glad I had an interfering Indian relative to knock some sense into my head.'

Yet not all NRI parents are lucky enough to have sensible advice dished out by Indian relatives. While most realise that the *laad pyaar* and pampering that goes on in child-centric India is just not possible abroad, they are still torn between the two cultures. It is one thing not being able to manage a feast for a two-year-old throwing a tantrum, it is quite another to feel guilty about it! Yet all the young NRI parents I have met, particularly the mothers, have spoken about the pulls and tugs of conflicting cultures. And this is strange because everyone in a rational frame of mind would agree that without domestic help, it is just not possible to pander to the child's every whim. The *beta raja* syndrome requires extreme attentiveness and devotion, which young NRI mothers, who still strive to be the best, lavish on their children.

NRI parents of an earlier generation were more practical. They ensured that their babies were born abroad (for passport purposes) and then transferred as infants to the grandparents' homes in India for a couple of years until they became 'manageable'. This strategy was seen as a workable option, with the children learning an Indian language and imbibing Indian values and culture, while the parents (often, both busy working professionals) got valuable time to concentrate on their careers or academics. There was complete trust in the Indian grandparents' bringing up of the baby, a total lack of guilt about the solution and everybody was happy. And judging by how the children turned out (young men and women in their twenties now—bright, ambitious, caring about the family and speaking Telugu, Tamil, Marathi or other regional languages fluently), this was a successful experiment.

There was an in-between solution too, not as extreme as the two-year, child-free holiday, but one that required the couple to spend a long time apart and the husband to miss out on the early months of the child's life. An NRI mum-to-be would travel to India in her seventh month of pregnancy (due to airline travel restrictions) and return six months later with her mother in tow to help out. Again, this was a uniquely Indian practical solution where the extended family pitched in and helped out.

With changing times, however, both births and early parenting are increasingly happening abroad. Practical issues and modern values dictate this growing trend. Mothers are often working till a fortnight before the birth of the child and often have to resume their careers within a few months after the baby is born. Modern fathers, too, want to be involved with early parenting and do not have enough leave to travel to India and live there for weeks. As a result, more and more NRI parents face the prospect of bringing up an infant outside India and it is amazing how little they are prepared for the cultural differences.

The modern literature on pregnancy, the ante-natal classes they attend, the parenting guides young NRI couples read—all look at birth and parenting through Western eyes. The advice is parent-centric and involves disciplining the child to suit the rhythm of modern Western life. The sooner the child is independent, the better it is for both parents and child. On the surface, all this appears fine. The young couple feel they are no different and their child will be brought up 'by the book'. However, once the baby is born and the latent cultural differences come into play, the young parents realise how Indian they are in their attitude to parenting. This is often reinforced by their own parents who come to help out and know only one way of parenting: the Indian way.

The advent of the internet, online mums' groups, Facebook forums and other networks often add to the pressure on the young couple. 'There are people on the net who seem to know it all' says one young dad I spoke to, 'I wish I could be as confident.' 'Not just that they know it all, they want to share it all,' adds his wife. 'It is hard enough balancing the two worlds (Indian and non-Indian) that we live in without the added dimension of the internet. There is just too much advice out there and by the time I have balanced out what Aunt Sarla says about *sua bhaji* and lactation with what the internet says, I begin to feel a bit dizzy!'

The plentiful advice is well meant, but often misplaced and results in several anomalies. Indian mums insist their daughters should not take the baby out of the house for fear of infection. Now this might make sense in India—but outside India, fear of infection is much lower and the practical need to shop for groceries makes many young mums step out just days after giving birth.

'I wish my unrelenting mum understood this,' says an NRI friend. 'I remember being trapped in the house for days while my husband shopped for all the wrong things at the supermarket!' She was talking about life in the US twenty years ago when her children were born and hopefully, online shopping will now solve this particular problem, but that is no excuse for not adapting to a new environment.

However, old Indian wives' tales survive and thrive—even in foreign lands. So I have seen young lactating mothers being force-fed all kinds of strange food items, such as huge bowls full of cumin and fenugreek seeds. They are not allowed to eat anything that will cause wind in the breastfeeding infant's stomach and certainly not spicy food. Interestingly, Western medical advice about matters like lactation is very neutral. Apart from urging plenty of fluid intake, they do not prescribe certain foods as better for lactation than others. A friend's daughter who recently had a baby at a British hospital tells an interesting story in this context. Just before checking out of the hospital, she asked the matron about what she should eat while breastfeeding and was surprised at the reply, clearly the official one. The matron in the hospital in south London said that it was illegal for them to comment on what food a breastfeeding mum should have as there is no conclusive medical evidence on what suits a lactating woman!

Like other NRI mums, I was no exception to the guilt-trip while I brought up children abroad. In fact,

I was forever caught in the comparison trap because Mahima's early parenting was in Mumbai while Ashima was brought up in the UK. Mahima's was a typical Indian upbringing: there were lots of relatives pitching in, the advantage of domestic help and high levels of social interaction—vegetable vendors at the door who spoke to 'Baby', horse-owners who gave her an extra five minutes of a ride free, restaurant waiters who had no qualms interrupting our meals to converse with our little one. She kept us awake at night because we could not bear to discipline her and she was fussy about her food. In short, she was a pampered little thing who manipulated her young and inexperienced parents to cater to her every whim and fancy. My husband used to walk her up and down the corridor for hours before she dozed off and no sooner did he put her down to sleep, she would wake up and cry again. Despite the help, we had a difficult time, as do most parents with a first-born.

We moved to the UK five months after Ashima was born, so by contrast, she was brought up at a lonely house in Surrey where I was the centre of her world and social interaction was very limited. In those harsh early days when I was run off my feet, I often joked that I had moved from one child and two maids in India to two children and no maid in the UK. A lot of the struggle I now realise, was self-inflicted. I tried to replicate Mahima's upbringing with Ashima. I tried to create an Indian universe around my new baby in a different country. If Mahima had had fresh vegetables cooked every mealtime, I was determined that Ashima should have the same. I would NOT, repeat NOT, give my baby frozen food. I was going to cook fresh food every day because I was an Indian mother and my baby deserved the best! So I scuttled about, miserable and worn thin with the effort—making *khichdi* at lunch time and single helpings of soup at dinner. I was suspicious of bottled baby food and experienced pangs of guilt every time I opened a jar. But time passed and the guilt lessened as my practical side took over. Ashima survived and thrived. After the initial cultural anxiety and comparison with Mahima's parenting, we brought her up with less fuss and she grew up fine! Like all second children, she had a golden temperament, slept better and ate much more than Mahima.

And while all this happened twenty years ago, my recent discussions with young mums show the desire for Indian pampering is still strong. A school friend's daughter who recently had a baby, came to spend a day with me last month and I was surprised to see that she cooked a single helping of *khichdi* in my kitchen! When I tried to give her the leftovers in a small plastic box, thinking she would be tired when she reached home, which was an hour's tube ride away, she said she never gives her seven-month-old leftovers. All meals are cooked by her and cooked fresh! She is an engineer from Cambridge University and holds an investment banking job. I suppose she applies all her high standards to child-rearing as well, but as a fond aunt I know how hard she must work to achieve the Indian ideal of fresh food at every meal and wish I could just tell her, 'Just relax, children grow up fine. Food stored in the fridge or freezer is not bad for the baby—you need to chill and so does the food!'

Similarly, I know of several young Indian couples who let the baby sleep in their bed for years and do not have social lives because they cannot bear to leave the baby alone—they think this is the best way to bring up a child abroad. It was the way they were brought up in India and they want to pass it on to their children in its unadulterated pure ghee form! This often puts a lot of strain on the parents, sometimes even on the marriage, and results in children who are less independent in the early years.

A friend who runs a day-care centre says the differences between Indian and non-Indian children are very striking. The non-Indian children are more bold and independent from a very early age. I could not help agreeing. I remembered noticing the emphasis on independence with Mahima and Ashima's playgroup friends, who were as little as three or four years old. They would come over to our house for a play date and after finishing their meal, ask me where the dishwasher was so they could put their plate away. That made me aware that it is never too early to inculcate good habits in children and my children were thereafter instructed to put away their plates too. I have to confess though, that before these children visited and impressed me, I was busy running around my own children, clearing up after them and generally thinking they were too young to help with housework. Clearly, I was the archetypal Indian mother right from the start!

One young mum I spoke to said that disciplining children the Western way was not approved of amongst Indian parents—she and her husband were the only Indian couple they knew of amongst their friends in London who had used Dr Ferber's method of sleep training, advocating that babies should soothe themselves to sleep. Since it involves letting the child 'cry it out' until he or she falls asleep, most of their Indian friends in London did not want to practise it. Now clearly, this is a cultural legacy as it goes against the grain of Indian parenting where the child is often rocked to sleep by various obliging relatives.

She said she had to steel herself to hear the child's piercing screams night after night and after two traumatic nights, begged her husband to employ professional help. He agreed, but seemed determined to go down the sleep training route because he had been to boarding school himself. So a professional sleep trainer was employed and sure enough, the child's crying decreased over successive nights and he learnt to sleep by himself without the aid of artificial props like rocking. While her child does not cry at bedtime any more, the cluck-clucking and disapproval of her Indian friends still rings in her ears. I can just hear them say what heartless parents we are, she laughs.

Kusumanjali Rabindranath, a young London mum of

two, has written a delightful book about her experience of putting her baby to bed. Called *Good Night and Good Luck*, it deals with the trauma of sleep training within the Indian cultural context. Influenced by her Italian neighbour whose son slept soundly from the age of three months, she decided to try the Gina Ford method of 'crying to sleep' without props for her sleepless baby and discovered she needed to train her mother too! Her Indian mother was aghast at the discipline required and did not accept the harshness of the exercise at all. Kusum, who sees herself as a hybrid, says she could see it from her mother's point of view; but on the other hand, the sleep deprivation was getting hard to bear and she felt she needed a smooth routine in her life.

While sleep training may elicit divided responses in both Indian and non-Indian homes (apparently, former British deputy prime minister, Nick Clegg, has gone public on his disagreement with his own wife over the Gina Ford method), certain bits of advice given by Western parenting guides and practitioners brook no debate whatsoever. They are clearly very difficult to follow in the Indian family set-up. Western parenting advice assumes a nuclear family while most Indian homes, especially in the days following a baby's birth, tend to admit the extended family into the parenting scene. 'One of the bits of advice that I found impossible to follow was the "skin to skin" bonding encouraged in the early days of the baby's life,' says a young friend. 'I could just see my mother-in-law's face blanch if she walked into my room and found me naked, pretending to be a kangaroo!' The vision still makes her break out into giggles and I could not help laughing too. So it was kaftans or nighties for this young mother instead.

Another young British Indian couple I met recounted how they were told very firmly during their ante-natal classes to not receive any visitors during the first few days. That was going to prove impossible, they realised, with uncles and aunts lining up on their doorstep every day. 'My mother has five siblings and my father has four,' the young man said, 'so there they were—welcoming the young grandniece into the fold. We would have been considered disrespectful and cold if we had followed the "No visitors" advice.'

A young mum remembers her home after the birth of her baby in Leeds. 'There were aunts suggesting names for the baby and what food a lactating mother should eat; there was a granduncle drawing up the astrological chart; there was my proud mum-in-law cooking for ten people every night. Not to speak of a masseuse and an aunt who made special corsets. We did not have the quiet bonding time with the baby that the hospital had recommended, but we sure had a party every night!'

As babies grow into toddlers, the relatives do not stop visiting. They come armed with books in Hindi, Gujarati, Tamil or whatever Indian language is used in that particular family. They bring CDs of Indian nursery rhymes or little *kurta-pyjama*s and *lehnga*s. They remind the toddlers and their parents that this is an Indian child in an Indian home—even if the land they live in is foreign.

All I can say in conclusion, is that you should feel blessed there are so many people out there looking out for you and your baby. So lap up the attention just as your child does and take the bits of advice you feel you can cope with.

SUMMARY

Cultural differences begin early in a baby's life—sleeping routines, feeding schedules or bathing techniques are all influenced by cultural perceptions.

NRI parents already juggling careers and child-rearing, may find the cultural asks of Indian child-centric upbringing very stressful. Understand and accept that.

Every generation has its own way of coping with child-rearing. NRI parents of an earlier generation solved this problem in a practical way: babies were sent to India and brought up by grandparents.

Maybe this generation of Indian parents has to come up with an innovative solution that works for them.

This could involve heeding only those bits of advice from Indian relatives that suit their lifestyle.

It could also mean that the Western literature on pregnancy and early childcare may have to be modified to suit Indian cultural values.

Be grateful for the involvement of the Indian family and use the strength of the family network to make the early years easier: for child-minding, for cooking meals for as well as educating and entertaining children.

4

CULTURE, ART AND HISTORY IN BITE-SIZE PORTIONS

Baaton Baaton Mein—Baat Ban Jaye!

Mohandas Karamchand Gandhi was at our table last night. He and Jawaharlal Nehru and other long-deceased (bless them) Indian freedom fighters have a habit of cropping up quite often at mealtimes actually. My parents take the whole thing of keeping us children 'rooted in India' quite seriously—quite a challenge since my sister and I have not lived in India since we were ten and eight respectively. Their indoctrination has included many years of weekend Hindi classes and lessons in Indian classical music and dance—some of which we have genuinely enjoyed; others we have silently and sometimes not-so-silently suffered. Yet the dining table crowns it all. Somehow they seem to think that generous helpings of chicken korma and dum aloo will help us imbibe the cultural/philosophy/history lessons on India and make them more palatable. I have to admit they do!

To get back to Gandhi—it all started with me announcing that I wanted to turn vegetarian. 'Why, isn't the chicken nice?' asked Mum, who despite being very oriented to Indian history tends to concentrate on the here and now mostly. 'Oh no, Mum,' I countered, 'it is not that at all. I have just thought about it deeply and I abhor the idea of meat festering in my digestive tract for forty-eight hours. Vegetarian food is easier to digest, and is more healthy.'

'Hmm…Gandhi was a vegetarian,' said my father in a tone that suggested a long monologue on Gandhi's eating habits was about to commence. Having had Gandhi as a dinner guest many more times than I would have cared to invite him to the table myself meant that I already knew a lot on the subject. The great man had been a vegetarian all his life, had become increasingly sparing in his diet with advancing age and lived mostly on goat's milk, fruit, nuts and leafy vegetables. When he was not fasting as a protest against British rule in India, that is. I, on the other hand, had no intention of giving up on vegetarian delights, such as chocolate profiteroles and ice cream sundaes.

'It is also environmentally friendly,' I added, eager to deflect the conversation from Gandhian asceticism. "I have read that it takes 78 calories of fossil fuel to produce one calorie of beef protein, but just one calorie of fossil fuel for one calorie of soya bean protein.' That

would clinch it for my environmentalist father, I thought. Not so.

'I am not convinced about soya bean cultivation actually,' he muttered. 'Large tracts of rainforest are being cleared in South America to grow soya bean, so the net environmental impact of eating soya bean may not be as good for the planet as was previously thought.'

'Eating as low as possible on the food chain is also a vindication of Gandhi's philosophy of non-violence,' I added, not about to give up easily.

'Yes, dear,' my mother interjected, 'but it must cover other areas of your life as well. You must occupy the moral high ground rather than resort to hate and violence in every confrontational situation. This was Gandhi's secret weapon—he shamed his enemies into submission.'

Hmm...I pondered silently. A vegetarian occupier of the moral high ground. That's what I wanted to be. Good on any CV, *in any century. 'Do you think Gandhi is still relevant, I mean, in this century?' I asked, just to reconfirm.*

'Absolutely,' said my father, 'he was a visionary when it came to issues like the environment. He once said, "The earth provides enough to satisfy every man's need, but not every man's greed." And this was before global warming and carbon credits and sustainable development were even dreamt of.'

'He was an all-time great,' added Mum. 'I think it was Martin Luther King who said, "Man learnt to think twice in our century, once with Einstein and then with Gandhi."'

I was impressed. Gandhi, it seemed, had it all: intellect, vision, moral fortitude. I wanted to be like him more than ever before.

'Did you know he experimented with eating beef during his youth; thought it would make him strong?' It was my father speaking—determined not to lose the thread of Gandhi's dietary habits. 'He came from the Gujarati bania caste and they are traditionally vegetarian, so it must have taken a lot of moral courage to eat not just any meat, but beef, which is actually forbidden to all Hindus.'

By now, with the enticing aroma of the chicken curry wafting towards me, I was thinking of another kind of courage at the opposite end of the scale: the courage it would require to be vegetarian. Besides, as I had learnt at the table today, there was so much more to Gandhi than vegetarianism.

'Well, I think I am going to follow Gandhi in more meaningful ways, rather than his diet,' I announced, shoving a large, but unsatisfactory, helping of vegetables into my mouth.

'Don't talk with your mouth full,' said Mum, spooning some chicken curry into my plate.

—Ashima writing on a dining table
conversation at home, 2007

There are very few Indians, even the most determined immigrants, who will quarrel with India's great cultural heritage and history. India has been home to

Mohenjodaro and Harappa, Ajanta and Ellora, the Qutub Minar and the Char Minar, the *dhrupad* and the *khayal*...it ranks right up there with Greece and Rome amongst ancient civilisations and is the birthplace of great religions. It has its own classical music and dance streams and has produced global stars such as Ravi Shankar and Zakir Hussain. Yet, knowledge of India in many NRI households is often gleaned from Bollywood films and little else. This is like American children living abroad thinking that Archie comics, and not Abraham Lincoln, somehow represent their country. Or, British kids growing up outside the UK being fed a diet of *EastEnders*, the British TV soap opera, and knowing nothing of the seafaring global power that once ruled more than half the world. Unthinkable! Yet NRI children are often woefully blank about Indian history, art and culture. A lack of teachers, time and inclination on the part of parents, exclude children growing up in these households from learning about and being proud of their roots. This is a shame.

It is time we started exploring India where its strengths lie—the history, music and dance and the great epics. It is time we told our children that learning the sitar or tabla is as cool as playing the guitar or drums. And that learning one instrument may actually help them master another one, from a different culture, easier. This is not to say that all NRI parents have neglected this aspect, just that on balance, I feel we are not vigilant enough to help our children imbibe the best of India.

In the US where I have several cousins, it is almost mandatory for girls to go to Bharatnatyam classes from an early age. The boys learn the violin or the tabla. Parents have organised networks and often clock up many miles taking their children to lessons during weekends already crowded with football practice and homework. Sometimes this zeal is influenced by the American desire to 'over-achieve', sometimes a genuine pride in the mother country, and sometimes just another qualification for a good university application, but whatever the motivation, it is highly commendable. American Indians are as organised about their 'cultural immersion' (I promise you, it *is* called that!) sessions just as they are with everything else. The parents take turns to drive the children for these lessons, they source good teachers and pool resources and time. NRIs in other countries have a lot to catch up on!

My own brushes with dance and music lessons were patchy. Mahima started on classical dance very late. She had been taken to a Bharatnatyam dance class very early on in Singapore, but reacted violently to the stern teacher who spoke or rather, shouted, all the time in an 'Amma' voice. She came back and announced she would never go again because the teacher was like Hitler and she hated her—she would never be able to learn under a dictator. I made some attempts to book folk dance lessons and even Bollywood dance classes and the girls, particularly Mahima I noticed, seemed to enjoy those. So when we got to the UK, I made one last ditch attempt. I enrolled her at the Bharatiya Vidya Bhavan for Kathak lessons. There, under the tutelage of a less stern male teacher, Mahima seemed to flower.

She looked forward to her classes, braved three changes on the tube, and never complained again. I don't think it was Bharatnatyam vs Kathak; it was the teacher who made the difference. So my learning has been, if your child reacts violently against an Indian dance or music class, do not insist on continuing. Try another class, another teacher. It may yet work. Remember, children growing up outside India are not used to the stern, authoritarian regime of an Indian school. Often, their reaction to the '*gurukul*' atmosphere has nothing to do with the fact that it is an Indian activity; it springs from being in an unfamiliar learning environment. Having said that, I was surprised to see Mahima bend down to touch her dance guru's feet as she entered her class at the Bharatiya Vidya Bhavan one day. When I asked her about it, she said breezily, 'That is the *parampara* (tradition).' Wow, I thought, that is a change!

Ashima learnt the tabla at the Bharatiya Vidya Bhavan in a class full of seventeen boys. She went to an all-girls school at the time and I am sure the boys in her tabla class added a great deal of excitement to her teenage years—whatever the reason, she enjoyed the classes and managed to learn without complaining. I did have to drive her there though because the tablas were heavy. So the other learning is—get your children to do less equipment-dependent activities if you don't like to drive!

I found myself having idli-dosa breakfasts with a set of dedicated mothers at the Bharatiya Vidya Bhavan on the weekends. I was a determined mother sure, but the dedication of some of the others was admirable. Some drove two hours to get to London, packed a breakfast which the children ate in the car and went back in the evening since different children had classes at different times during the day. One enterprising mother had signed up for Hinduism classes at the Bhavan that kept her occupied for some of the many hours she spent there.

There are Indian parents I know whose children have successfully learnt a Western musical instrument or done ballet up to a high level and achieved much success. Whether it is the piano or ballet, if your child is enjoying the experience, the golden rule of all good parenting (and Indian parenting is no different), is to encourage them to continue. Little is achieved by imposing Indian music or dance lessons. All I am asking is that exposure to Indian classical music and dance is a good idea and given the right teacher and class ambience, it can work.

In fact, exposure to India generally works much better if it is part of everyday living. A child picks up more information through dining table conversations, music playing in the house, film choices made for the family and parental attitudes to the mother country than you can imagine. Children, as we already know, 'Do as you do', not 'Do as you say'. So if they find that the parents reminisce about India fondly or talk in animated terms about India's status as an emerging country, they will be eager to learn more. Ashima had obviously picked up a lot of knowledge about Gandhi through her father's admiration for the great man. She was never actively engaged in the conversation until she was much older but she was obviously listening…and learning.

On the other hand, if children find the parents talk about the collapsing infrastructure and potholes of India after every holiday and their limited engagement with India is Bollywood films, they will imbibe a very superficial view of the country. I can never forget a startling instance of this warped view that came from a second-generation British Indian girl whom I interviewed for the post of a Communications Manager at the London-based Indian charity I worked for. The charity raises funds and sends them to Pratham—one of India's well-known education NGOs—which is doing a remarkable job on reaching out to underprivileged children.

The interviewee was pleasant enough, had been born and brought up in London and was well educated. We seemed to get along fine. Then I asked her which of India's problems she would fix if she got the chance to be prime minister. It was the last question, designed to elicit an easy wrap-up answer. I heard her say 'education' in my head even before I had finished asking the question. (Come on, she was being interviewed for a job with an education NGO!) She paused, then wrinkled her pretty nose and said, 'The litter definitely…India is so, so dirty.' I was stunned at the time but on reflection, I can see why she said it. Her attitudes were shaped by what she had heard her parents talk about at the dining table! This is not to say India is not dirty, this is about how parental attitudes towards India can influence the way your children think.

So being responsible when you discuss India with your children does help. Sure, point out the warts, discuss the litter, criticise the infrastructure, but also come up with informed solutions. Put the current poverty of India in historical perspective. India has been a rich, civilised and more advanced country than many European countries or America for 1,800 out of the 2,000-odd years of human history. Point out that 500 years can change everything and how colonial rule affected India, for instance. In 1500, the most influential and important cities in Europe were Constantinople and Prague, not London and Paris. I used the historical card a great deal because my parenting was before India became a potential superpower. Today's NRI parents have the whole emerging economy argument to present.

Take time to rebut the common perceptions about India that children often come across at school or in the media in an informed and rational way. Yes, occasionally there are cows on the street, but there are also over 23,000 kilometres of super high speed highways. Or, arranged marriages do not equal forced marriages and are no different from dating websites because interests and background are matched up in the same way. Both the boy and girl have a choice. And yes, these marriages actually work! Dowry is an evil, yes, but it has been legislated against by the Indian parliament. In fact, the Indian government is doing a lot to help women. The parliament has recently given girls the right to family property and a bill has been tabled to ask for reservation of seats in parliament for women, which will take the percentage of women representing constituencies to 33 per cent—higher than that of the UK, which currently stands at 25 per cent. India has had a female speaker in the parliament and a woman prime minister as well as President. I could go on and on—but you get the idea. There is always more than one way to look at India, so make sure your children get a balanced perspective.

And finally, don't ever forget to discuss the many positives that India offers. An important example is the warmth of family life and relationships. During one family holiday to India, I remember pointing out to the children that so many inter-generational family groups could be seen eating out together in India, compared to the West, where one sees only couples or at most, the nuclear family. I linked it to the fact that the extended family is alive and well as a concept. The girls looked disinterested and did not respond. I was therefore, really surprised to note that next summer, when my parents visited us in London and we were eating out, the girls brought up this point. They looked around the Italian restaurant where we were enjoying a meal and said to my parents, '*Nana, Nani*, see, nobody else has come with their grandparents!' They had remembered. So discuss and debate all things Indian. Use the Taj Mahal, use Sachin Tendulkar, use A.R. Rahman, use Mahatma Gandhi; use whatever it takes to engage, interest and enliven the conversation. The points made will stick in their minds!

SUMMARY

NRI children often grow up without much knowledge of India's rich art, history and culture. This is a shame, because this is India's strength and we should take pride in it.

Cultural immersion is easier and more practical if like-minded Indian parents join hands. Persuade your friends to scout for Indian classes and car pool to take them; the kids will enjoy it too.

Children often react against unfamiliar learning environments and sometimes, Indian language classes or music classes tend to have a different ambience from the schools the children are used to. The answer is to persist—try another class, another teacher.

Even casual dining table conversations can shape your children's views on India. Be conscious that children are always listening and absorbing. Discuss India's art and music if you want to raise cultural connoisseurs. Discuss only potholes and you leave a gaping hole in your child's knowledge of one of the world's greatest civilisations!

5

MAID IN MANHATTAN

When Does Indian Parenting Stop, if Ever?

It's hard work being a mum in a strange city with a fridge and a larder that stocks all manner of eclectic foods such as quinoa, agave nectar and soy milk and absolutely no chillies, normal milk, instant coffee or anything remotely delicious. Today is the first day when I have not been requisitioned to take the dry cleaning out or get medicines for the cats (statins no less) or any other outdoor errands so am 'resting' with only ten people invited for dinner! Went and shopped for normal food items like chicken and lamb and they are nestling on the stove top right now amongst hopes that my daughter's friends will actually eat regular food. I dread to think what might happen this evening if they demand tofu lettuce wraps instead!

I had an interesting encounter at Carnegie Hall the other day. Since I had spilt some tea on a pair of concert tickets, which I had used as coasters while trying to save the table from getting cup-base stains, I was informed by my irate offspring that the concert tickets were more valuable than the table (only IKEA and hence to be thrown away in a few months); therefore, I should make amends by offering to go to Carnegie Hall and get duplicates issued. After queuing up, I arrived, flustered, at the ticket window with my strange request: could I please have some duplicates in exchange for the sodden mess I was holding? When I explained why, the man at the counter asked if I had my daughter's ID. So I got even more flustered and said I didn't, but he could check mine; I had a driver's licence with the same surname. At that point he smiled and said it's fine, no one except a mum would bother to take this kind of trouble to placate her child. So I got my duplicate tickets and we traded knowing smiles about mothers and children!

On the plus side, I bought some caffeinated tea bags when I went shopping this morning and was enjoying my first decent cup of tea with some shortbread I had brought along from London as a gift for Mahima's friends (silly me, how could I even think they eat shortbread?). When we welcome our innocent babies into this world, little do we know we are signing up to a life of bondage, happily and smilingly forever! Happy Mother's Day!

—Email written to my friends from New York,
May 2012

We went on holiday to the Andalucia region of Spain one year during the mid-term break and took one of Ashima's friends along. She was Emma, an English girl from Essex, tall, blonde and already very beautiful and self-assured at fifteen. We had a very lovely holiday where we took in the grandeur of the Alhambra Palace and travelled to the fortified village of Sante Fe across the mountains, imbibing Moorish history and the Christian crusades all along the journey. The girls joined in quite happily, marvelling at the architecture and harking back to history lessons at school.

On our last day, we had a quiet dinner at a charming restaurant in one of the beautiful *pueblos blancos* (white villages) that dot the Andalucia region. The girls were allowed to drink a bit of wine and we were all very relaxed. I took the opportunity to ask Emma about her experience of being on holiday with an Indian family. Was it different from what she might have experienced with her own family?

'Yes,' she replied unhesitatingly. 'We would have gone to the beach and sunned ourselves the whole time!' Of course, there was the beach and the entire southern coastline of Spain! But it had never once crossed our minds that it was anything more than passing scenery. Pavan doesn't even swim and the last thing I wanted to do was sunbathe when there were historical and architectural delights to be discovered. It was too late to take Emma to the beach and certainly too late to get her the tan she was expecting to have at the end of a holiday in Spain. So I gave her a lengthy explanation of how Indians and other Asian cultures value fair skin and why skin-lightening creams are a major seller in Asia—which she listened to very carefully.

Later, when the conversation had moved on to other things like packing for tomorrow's flight and I was telling Ashima that she must give me all her toiletries to pack or they would leak into her clothes, Emma spoke again. 'There is one more difference,' she said thoughtfully, 'You treat Ashima very differently from how my mother treats me.' 'How?' I asked eagerly, sensing I was on the cusp of making an important cultural difference discovery. 'I don't know,' she hesitated, trying to choose her words carefully. 'You treat her like...she is...much younger than she is.' There, she had said it! The honest truth of her words hit home. It was not said as a teenage rebellion statement, nor was it judgmental. It was just what she said it was—a cultural difference between parenting styles.

This was my first realisation that I did things differently from my Western counterparts in the children's teenage years. In all the hurly-burly of early parenting, I had not analysed my parenting style to see if it had evolved over time. Of course, I had progressed somewhat: from the 24x7 intensive care that a baby requires to the supervision of a toddler to the help with homework and choice of subjects for GCSEs stage. But obviously, the motherly concern (some would call it irritation) in my voice had not altered to suit a more appropriate form of address for older children. The strong desire to control the environment so my baby didn't come to harm had not mellowed. Was I some shrewish mother about to stunt my children's growth forever? Would they grow up tied to my saree *pallu,* unable to function as mature adults? There is obviously a time to stop taking charge, cleaning up after them and letting them learn from their mistakes. With my youngest now fifteen, perhaps it was time to let go. After all, Emma's busy mother, a doctor, seemed to have brought up a mature, considerate and thinking young lady without making her feel like a baby.

Most people, including Westerners, would agree that parenting never ends. Once you are a parent, you are conditioned to worry about, care for and delight in your 'little one' no matter how old they are. However, it is clear in most Western parents' minds that having brought up their children, made them independent both emotionally and financially, it is time to enjoy 'me-time'. They feel no guilt in taking expensive holidays, pursuing old hobbies or starting new ones and downsizing their home to suit themselves. The relationship with the children dwindles to a few phone calls, the structured Mother's Day and Father's Day lunches and Christmas, though even that by all accounts, is disappearing. Some girls maintain close relationships with their mothers and seek their help with childcare, but again, it is with ample consideration for their mother's time. I have an English friend who helps out twice a week with her daughter's children while she goes out to work. The daughter does a four-day work week and the other two days are taken care of by paid childcare. 'This arrangement works well,' says my friend, 'because it is fair to everyone.' She does her two days happily and willingly, loves her grandchildren dearly, but would never dream of becoming a total substitute for paid childcare. Nor does she think of how much her daughter would save if she did not pay for the child-minder.

With Indian parents, however, it is much harder to draw the line. The desire to see the children achieve success in their careers, be financially comfortable and bring up the perfect grandchildren is sometimes so passionate that it results in inequitable and untenable situations. It is worth noting here that many NRIs return to India to retire while the children continue to live abroad. So you get situations where the wife seems to spend six months of the year abroad looking after the grandchildren, while the poor husband is left to his own devices—playing bridge or golf at the club and making his annual fifteen-day trip to see the children.

I even know a couple in India who give up whatever they are doing between 8 p.m. and 9 p.m. every evening because that is the time (in the US) when their daughter drives to work (morning EST) and is unable to keep an eye on the child-minder. Once she gets into the office and switches on the screen, which beams the camera feed from her home and her eagle eye on the child-minder is restored, the grandparents can relax and go back to their daily diet of Zee TV soaps, which though bizarre, are nothing quite like this situation! Technology is now being employed to bridge the physical distance and provide support to the child! Indian parenting *zindabad*!

When asked why Indian parents go to such lengths, the answers are straightforward. 'We have educated our daughter and it would be a shame to see her sit at home and take care of the children, so we help out in any way we can.' Or, 'These days, with the economy being so unstable, it is important that both our son and daughter-in-law work, so we do our share.'

There are, of course, some Indian parents who think like Westerners, but they are not the norm. Like Mrs Desai whose Harvard-educated son and daughter-in-law have part-time jobs because they both take turns staying at home and minding the children. She does not like staying for months in another home, never mind if it is her own son's. They would never make it to the Indian Grandparents Honour Roll. I can almost hear the whispers: Na...who do they think they are? What selfish parents! Their children will also learn this attitude. Who will come and look after them in their old age? As you sow, so shall you reap and so on...The list of naysayers is as long as it is vicious. But surely the senior Desais are entitled to their own way of life. I don't think they are trying to be Indian or Western, it is just what works for them.

The ideal Indian parent-adult child relationship seems to be one of never-ending dependency on the part of the child and the desire to feel needed on the part of the parent—particularly mothers. Life abroad brings its own twists and turns to this unfolding soap. For example, some visiting mothers arrive at adult children's nests—pronounce them unclean and unfit for human habitation. They then get down to work with vacuum cleaners and mops and produce a neat home, which the child barely notices but brings great pleasure to the mother. The more posh mothers pay for expensive visits by professional cleaners. However it is done, cleanliness and order is restored and the parent leaves with that satisfying sense of achievement. The children have a bemused 'you know what Mum's like' attitude while they eye the freezer full of Indian food which the mother has left behind.

I even know someone who photographed all the plastic boxes of *palak paneer* and *kali dal* she had cooked and placed in her adult working son's freezer in New York and put it up as a cover photo on Facebook. How did we know it was *palak paneer*? The marker pen lovingly used to inscribe each box helped! I am sure the 126 likes for the photo from admiring friends helped reassure her that she was doing something right.

I am guilty of these secret and not-so-secret pleasures as well. During a recent visit to the girls, I emptied out the kitchen shelves, wiped each bottle with a disinfectant wipe and placed it back. Whether my order made any sense to the girls or not, or how long it would last, made no difference to the enthusiasm with which I approached the task. I had a free morning and thought it was the perfect way to spend it. I could have spent it at the

Museum of Modern Art two blocks down the road, but much as I like Piet Mondrian's symmetry, it did not compare with the neatly lined bottles of spices in my children's kitchen!

On another day, I attempted ironing and when that was stymied by the two cats we were cat-sitting, jumping up on to the ironing board, I actually took photos of them and put them up on Facebook. So was I being unreasonable? Not respecting the way my children wanted to live (in an expedient way mostly, which entailed no ironing of clothes), or as Ashima's friend had pointed out, was I treating my children like babies? I think I was guilty of all of the above in the Western sense but as the forty-six likes from my friends (mostly Indian) on Facebook suggested, I was only being a good Indian mother of adult children. And that entails undying love, unending care and constant cooking, cleaning and ironing.

What about the children then? Are they grateful? Do they realise there is a cultural difference operating here? I think, by and large, they do. I know a young man who is studying medicine in the US and is frank about his cultural advantage. 'I would be buried under a mountain of debt if I had Western parents because they would expect me to take loans for my education. Luckily, I have Indian parents with generous hearts and deep pockets!' The father, a doctor in the US himself, certainly now earns enough to fund his son's eight-year stint at Ivy League medical colleges but his own struggle to reach where he has, is not held up as an example to be emulated. His own journey to the US, via a relatively low paying job as an National Health Service doctor in the UK and dotted with numerous exams and challenges at every level is considered worthy, but not worth repeating. His children do not have to come up the hard way. 'Do you not think we Indians spoil our children?' I once asked his wife. 'Of course, we do,' she replied unhesitatingly, 'Why shouldn't we? They are good children, they produce good academic results, they work hard, they deserve it.' In her mind, as long as the money was being spent on education and not being blown up on partying by irresponsible brats, there was no better use for it.

In the children's minds too—as long as they achieve good results, they are repaying their parents concern. Later on, as they go on to get jobs, these children, spoilt with loving care and endless money for academics, tend to spoil their parents in turn. Since the parents don't need basics like televisions and fridges, the latest computer gadgets are gifted or expensive holidays planned for the parents. Buoyed up by Bollywood films and television commercials that stress the same family values, a new generation of Shravan Kumars is born. This time the parents may not need to be carried around on baskets like Shravan did but hey, a pair of wheels in the driveway is a good idea. I have a cousin whose son made her a supplementary credit card holder as soon as he acquired an investment banking job in London. She came to visit me in Singapore and went on a shopping spree that was fully paid for by her dutiful offspring.

The numerous advertisements aimed at young adults on Indian channels reflect this concern for parents is widely prevalent. There is a charming Mastercard TV commercial that talks of tickets to Disney World being $240, the flights to Florida being such and such and ends with a close-up shot of an old couple on a roller coaster and the triumphant sign off 'Watching your parents become children again—priceless!' It captures the Indian ethos perfectly. Indian children are meant to look after their parents and use their money to fund a comfortable old age. This may or may not happen in reality, depending on the parents' financial circumstances, but by and large, this is the aspirational model and in a media-driven world, this happy family certainly exists.

So is the worry about their own old age the motivating factor when it comes to the never-ending parental care that Indian parents provide for their children? I would like to think not. In the case of NRI parents particularly, the economic factors rarely come into play. The parents are normally comfortably off and the children certainly do not have to provide financial support. It is driven by cultural factors such as 'keeping the family together' and 'reminding the children who they are and where they come from'. One family I know actually invites their married children along on two expensive holidays each year to keep family ties. The lady scours *Condé Nast Traveller* for the latest, most exotic and luxurious break she can find and justifies the expense to herself as the cost of communicating with adult children. 'You have to make it attractive for them,' she rationalises, 'Remember, they live in the Western world where going for holidays with Mum and Dad is NOT COOL.' The expensive African Safari holiday may take the edge off peer disapproval, but it makes me squirm to think that the only reason the 'kids' go for holidays with their parents is the fact that it is free.

It also made me wonder if, in fact, adult NRI children are the ultimate pampered children in a world that seems to have spawned an entire Peter Pan generation. The Peter Pan generation—in their late twenties and thirties—is a generation that simply refuses to grow up. Their parents are tail-end baby boomers who are the most prosperous of all generations in recent history. As post-war industrialisation led to the prosperity and boom of the '50s and '60s and then the finance and internet boom starting in the '80s and right up to the crash of 2008, unprecedented amounts of wealth were created. This led to rich, overprotective helicopter parents, who hovered around children (shades of Indian mothers here!) and ended up raising a generation of pampered young adults.

While the parents worked hard, married relatively early and had no problem accepting responsibility, their children delay marriage and other responsibilities and often return to live at home with parents after a brief and expensive foray into independent living. The rising cost of living and the insecurity in the job market have both contributed to this phenomenon and there are now a large number of Western young adults living with their parents. However, this is seen as a temporary and unhappy arrangement.

In the Indian sphere, however, it is a fortuitous way to extend the parenting and protecting. Indian parents living in the Western world often keep young adult children at home on the grounds that they can save for their first home or because jobs are so uncertain. In a world which seems to be reinforcing an 'Indian' way of life, why not enjoy a few more years with the children and make sure the *bachcha*s get a firm footing in life? That seems to be the Indian parents' refrain!

Which brings me to the point that, like all relationships, the NRI parent and adult child relationship is a two-way street, with the children being reasonably happy spending time with their parents whether on holiday or living with them and chipping in with emotional or financial support, if needed. I met a young man in New York recently who told me that he would only marry an Indian girl because a Westerner would never understand his close relationship with his mother. As she was divorced early, the mother and son have been through hard times together so he obviously feels responsible for her, which was lovely to see. On her part, she never re-married, devoted her youth to bringing him up devotedly and still keeps one room for him in an expensive two-bedroom apartment in New York, even though he has moved out. Is that too close for comfort? Abnormal? By Western standards, maybe. If they had been a standard Western mother and son, she may have re-married, possibly divorced again; he would have had step-siblings, not the expensive education he enjoyed and certainly not the unique and very special relationship he enjoys with his mum today as a result of the brave journey they took together. Am I being facile here? Perhaps, but the idea of a great *ma-beta* story is the stuff of which legends and Bollywood films are made!

SUMMARY

Western parenting is aimed at making the children financially and emotionally independent by the time they are young adults.

Indian parenting, on the other hand, is about never-ending dependency on the part of the child and the desire to be needed on the part of the parents. However, instead of beating up ourselves over this—let us celebrate the difference.

The desire to see our adult children succeed in the world and bring up the perfect grandchildren, often drives Indian parents to selfless extremes.

By and large, adult Indian children are grateful for the financial and emotional support they receive—right through life. They, in turn, pamper the parents with expensive gifts and take care of their needs in old age.

Strong family ties are one of the blessings of being Indian so we should be happy and grateful for them. If you are an NRI child, accept your parents' involvement—they really care for you, even if they sometimes come across as interfering by Western standards.

If you are an Indian parent, keep doing what you have to—you will be unhappy if you conform to standards dictated by another culture to stop being involved in your children's lives.

6

THE IMPORTANCE OF TEACHING AN INDIAN LANGUAGE

Hindi Hain Hum... Vatan Hai Hindustan Hamara

Scene: A bedroom in an Indian household on a Sunday morning. Noises of a pressure cooker whistle heard in the background

Characters:

Girl 1 (ten-year-old)

Girl 2 (eight-year-old)

Mother (with urgency in voice): Come on girls, Ashaji will be here any minute—get out of bed.

Girl 1 (mumbling): Five minutes more...

Mother (raising her voice): She will be here in five minutes…come on. You have to get dressed too.

Girl 2 (sleepily): She is always late.

Girl 1 (giggling): Indian Standard Time, Mummy—you said so yourself!

Mother (sternly): I am not interested in whether she comes late or not. I do NOT want you to be late.

Girl 1 sits up in bed.

Girl 1 (cheekily): Mummy…you always like everything Indian, so what's wrong with Indian Standard Time?

Mother (smiles in spite of herself): *Chalo, chalo*, I don't want any smart comments.

Girl 2 (speaking from under the duvet): I don't like her—she smells.

Mother: That is a BAD thing to say. Ashaji is your Hindi teacher and she uses hair oil, which a lot of Indian people do.

Girl 2 (still under duvet): Yuck! And she speaks English all funny.

Girl 1 (excitedly): Mummy, how about we teach her English instead?

Mother (back to stern tone): This is unacceptable. Do you speak about your other teachers like this? No!

Girl 1 (defiantly): Our school teachers do not have two cups of tea and ask for biscuits in the classroom.

Girl 2 (sitting up at last): Or talk to their children all the time on their mobile phones!

Mother (attempting patience): Ashaji comes to the home so she has to be treated like a guest and also she has no childcare, so it is important for her to speak to her children. She is a very good Hindi teacher and you will be glad you know Hindi one day. Come on, my *raja beta*s... quick, let's get ready.

Girl 1 (disappearing into bathroom): Why are you calling us *beta*? It is *beti*. We know that much Hindi.

Girl 2 (diving into duvet again): It's not FAIR. Jessica is having a birthday party at the zoo and I have to go late because of her. I hate her. I hate Hindi and I hate you! *Mujhe Hindi nahi seekhna hai!*

Mother (whisking off duvet): *Nahi seekhni hai*! When will you EVER get the gender thing?

Much as it may sound amusing written down and in the past, it *is* a struggle—always difficult to make children living in an alien environment realise and appreciate that India is relevant to their lives, that the knowledge of an Indian language is an important life-skill or an essential part of their identity. And that they will actually thank you one day for persisting with familiarising them with the language.

A lot of my early parenting was done in the years before India became 'cool'. In the early '90s, when Mahima turned up at her local playgroup in the UK with no knowledge of English (we had spoken to her only in Hindi at home for three years), the teacher looked horrified, pronounced she would be confused trying to speak both languages and made me sit outside the class for a whole week in case she had trouble communicating with Mahima! Remember, this was in the days before mobile phones so I had no choice.

Besieged by self-doubt about my rash neglect of the environment my child was growing up in, worried that she would cry and feel lonely in a sea of foreign faces and a strange tongue, I had little choice.

So I arrived at the playgroup with a confused Mahima, a book I had been trying to read for months and a toddler (Ashima), who would constantly try and enter the playgroup and whom I would constantly have to shush. It was both uncomfortable and humiliating. On the first day of the playgroup, sitting there with my unread book in my hands and trying to amuse Ashima for three hours in a darkened church entrance area (the playgroup used to function in a church hall), many gloomy thoughts passed through my mind. I wondered whether the teacher would have behaved similarly with a German or French mother whose child did not know English. I wondered (briefly) whether I should change family policy for Ashima and start on some English with her. But then my determination to keep my children as

Indian as I possibly could, re-asserted itself. I dug in my heels and called the wandering Ashima. 'Come and listen to your favourite story about the crow and the fox,' and as she settled into my lap, another informal lesson in Hindi began!

The next day, I had some respite in the form of company; another mother had been asked to stay back because her son had cried the whole day before that and wanted his mother. The English lady said she had been having problems with her son since she had recently separated from her husband. I was suitably sympathetic and assured her all would be fine eventually. When she learnt of my story she looked horrified! 'How come your daughter doesn't speak English?' she asked incredulously, 'You seem to be extremely fluent.' I had to explain that we wanted our children to speak both Hindi and English and the only shot at Hindi we would get were in the pre-school years. She appreciated the logic, but remained convinced that Mahima would have serious difficulties mastering English. I did not bother to contradict her—being bi-lingual myself, I knew how easy it is to switch from one language to another. And sure enough, within a month Mahima was speaking non-stop in English! Ashima who always copied anything Mahima did or said, thus had a smattering of English in her vocabulary before she arrived at the playgroup two years later.

So was that the end of the story? Not at all! Starting children on Hindi is one thing, keeping it up quite another. Once the outside world creeps in—in the form of school, television and non-Indian playmates, children tend to keep the Hindi they know firmly in the comprehension box. That is, they understand when spoken to in Hindi, but reply in English. And since the parents know English, the automatic progression is that when replied to in English, the parent then switches to English as well. Gradually, over the years, the habit of speaking in the Indian language be it Tamil, Telugu, Marathi or Hindi, dies down within the family. Over the years, I have met many NRI parents who have lamented the fact that their schoolgoing children have completely forgotten their early childhood Hindi.

So is there a way to keep the language alive in a fun and interesting way? Trips to the mother (tongue) country, Hindi classes, Bollywood films, Hindi tuition at home, we tried it all with varying results.

Frequent trips to India did help in the early years and I remember my children coming back from long summer holidays in India completely fluent in Hindi. But as they grew older and their accent sounded noticeably different from that of friends and family they met, they became shy about speaking in Hindi, even in India. The arrival of Katrina Kaif, the British Indian Bollywood actor, didn't help. From speaking 'funny', their accent was labelled 'Katrina Kaif' by their Indian cousins. The fact that this NRI girl now rules the Bollywood film industry despite her stilted Hindi was lost on my girls who, like all young people in an alien environment, wanted to conform to their peer group above everything else and that included speaking and sounding like their peers. It took them many years and some growing up to realise that a trip to India is a long, enjoyable lesson in Hindi where they can practise their language skills, make mistakes and improve—without anyone thinking they were strange!

Formal language classes is another way to keep up the language with schoolgoing children. Most countries with a high density of an Indian population do offer parents the opportunity to access learning Indian languages for their children. But like anything else, it requires commitment from the parents. I remember Saturday and Sunday mornings in Singapore being entirely swallowed up by Hindi classes, which were held near the Sikh gurdwara on Serangoon Road. It meant giving up two precious mornings when we could have done other fun things as a family. I was working full-time so it meant giving up valuable 'me-time' as well, but my determination never wavered. I would loiter around the school compound, sit under a tree and read a book (not pleasant in over 30 degrees) or do my weekly Indian shopping along the shops on Serangoon Road. Slowly, as I became friends with equally determined mothers, we used to have lovely idli-dosa breakfasts in Little India together and chat. They were simple women whose husbands worked in Singapore. They came from fairly traditional backgrounds in India and little had changed in their accent or appearance. Their children went to local Singapore government schools, not elite international schools, and the only reason they brought their children to this Hindi class was their determination that their children must know Hindi and be proud of their Indian heritage. Their children were a bright bunch who were encouraged to opt for Mandarin in their school as they felt that knowing the local language would help them get better jobs.

What struck me as particularly interesting was that not all the parents were native Hindi-speakers. There were Maharashtrians who had been unable to find a suitable Marathi class and had opted for the convenience of the Hindi School instead. There were even a couple of south Indians. It is amazing how these regional differences evaporate when we leave India. Standing outside the Hindi School in Singapore, bound by a common feeling of belonging to India, it is hard to imagine the bigotry and narrow-mindedness that still exists in India, that only a few decades ago the introduction of Hindi led to riots in Chennai and Hindi films could not be shown!

While the barriers are slowly coming down, there is still a long way to go. Chetan Bhagat's bestselling book, *Two States,* about inter-community marriage is hilarious, but makes a serious point about modern India. Even amongst educated Indians—and we are talking about people whose children go to elite education institutions like the Indian Institutes of Management (IIMs)—there are myths and misconceptions about other Indian communities. The Punjabis look down on the spartan south Indians while the south Indians turn up their noses at the vulgar north Indians. And yet, outside a school in

Singapore, a Tamil mother chats with a Punjabi mum as they discuss where to buy the best *bhindi* and *lauki* in Singapore ☺.

It is noteworthy that none of my husband's banking colleagues' children came to this school. So is Hindi considered not so cool among some Indians? Is it a 'class' situation? Are other mothers more modern than I am? I remember a dinner party where I was talking about the struggles of keeping up Hindi in the family and one banker's wife saying quite loftily that she and her husband did not bother because their children (in the American School at the time) would never return to India. As it happens, fifteen years later, both her son and daughter are now living and working in India! The son graduated from his American university, hated his first job in the US and returned to run an innovative art fund in India. The daughter met and married an Indian boy studying in the US and he returned to help with his family business. Were this couple just not aware of where the world was going? Well, they were not alone.

Remember, even fifteen years ago, the press reports on India were not positive. The BRIC report, which put the Indian economy into the exclusive club of future economic powerhouses, was not published by Goldman Sachs until 2001 and certainly did not become common parlance until several years later. Indians who had left the country and were giving their children a top class international education were preparing their children to do the same—that is, live outside India. They were, in fact, so proud that their children would have all the advantages they never had, like an Ivy League degree or an MBA from Harvard, that they would never have to go back to India again. They had to be schooled instead in the ways of the West: ballet classes, riding lessons, piano—but Hindi, good God, why?

Personally, I don't think I ever thought of Hindi as a career tool or a life skill. For me it was an integral part of an Indian identity and I thought it was my duty to hand it down to my children. I never thought of India as good or bad, or better or worse than any other place. It was and always will be, a special place called HOME. And Hindi was the language spoken in this special place. But it's amazing how many NRI parents give up without even trying and justify it to themselves in many different ways. 'We tried, but once they went to school, they never looked back.' 'I am Gujarati and my husband is Punjabi so we could never decide which language they should speak.' 'Oh, I was never very good at Hindi myself, I always got the worst marks in Hindi.' But for every NRI parent who gives up, there is another who goes to amazing lengths. Like the couple I know who diligently invite their parents to stay with them for many long months in a year and speak to the children ONLY in Hindi. Or those who don't let their children put on the English subtitles when they watch Bollywood films.

The children's reaction to learning an Indian language is often quoted as an excuse for not pursuing it. Yes, NRI children do not think learning an Indian language is great fun. It is most often an activity thrust on them in an environment that offers many other attractive diversions. The books are not as interesting as those they get in their regular school. The content is completely alien to them, not having grown up in India. I remember Mahima and Ashima struggling with words like *dhobi* (washerman) or *lakkadhara* (person who fells trees). These were professions completely unknown to them, since they'd grown up with a washing machine that did the washing and were told by an environmentalist father that felling trees was bad. 'Why don't the police catch all the *lakkadharas*, Mummy?' a bewildered Mahima had asked once, not being able to reconcile this information with her environmental conscience.

Alas, the content of Hindi books for children left a lot to be desired. I am pretty sure it was the same in other regional languages. To expect that children are going to be entertained by stories of Pappu brushing his teeth and wearing clean clothes and not having lice in his hair is hardly the stuff of which childhood fantasies are made. Yet, basic level Hindi books some twenty years ago were not very interesting. I see from websites that certain strides have been made and I hope Indian parents will now have an easier time. And why not? Indian literature has a lot to offer—we have stories from the *Panchatantra*, we have the Ramayana and the Mahabharata, we have Akbar and Birbal. However, if the path to reading and enjoying these is made more accessible in the form of widely available well-published books and well-produced DVDs, I am sure more parents will embark on the journey. There are now, of course, apps that teach Hindi and several other less tedious ways than going to Hindi class, but like much else in life, learning a language requires time, effort and patience.

Both my children went on to learn Hindi at the university level as a foreign language. It was taught from scratch and hence a very easy credit! 'The easiest three credits I've earned,' said Mahima, thanking me—many years later. It also helped her during a work stint in Mumbai where she quarrelled with taxi drivers fluently! Who knows what the future holds for them, but they both look back on the arduous Hindi classes they endured all through their childhood with fond affection and are very happy they know enough Hindi to get by.

I stress the importance of language because it is a direct link to the culture of the country. Hindi/Urdu is a gateway to the enjoyment of Begum Akhtar's *ghazal*s, to the understanding of the *Raas Leela* being expressed through dance and music, to *thumri*s, to Hindustani classical music. For someone who knows Bengali, there is a whole new world of Rabindranath Tagore's poetry and Satyajit Ray films to discover, which translations and subtitles just do not convey in the same way. Similarly, there is great literature in Tamil and some groundbreaking theatre in Marathi to be enjoyed if one knows the language. Our children may or may not wish to take the adventure further, but as Indian parents, if we equip them with the basic tool kit, they will surely be thankful as adults.

SUMMARY

It is a struggle to make children living outside India understand the relevance and importance of being fluent in an Indian language.

Start early, in the pre-school years. If both parents don't speak the same Indian language, let one parent speak to the child in his/her language.

Make sure the early advantage is not lost—once the child goes to school, replace the informal learning with formal classes in the language learnt during pre-school.

If there are no classes available locally, make sure there are books, films, tapes, CDs and other equipment that the child gets exposure to.

All trips to India, especially over extended summer holidays, can be used to further language skills. Enroll the children for language classes during the holidays. Bring back a stack of CDs and DVDs each time you go to India.

With online shopping, better and more interesting content on Indian language educational tools, and better communications and connectivity, you are far better off than we were twenty years ago. Think lessons on Skype, think talking with grandmothers on Facetime; the possibilities to practise the language are endless!

7

ACADEMICS WITH AN A+

Followed by Career$ with a Dollar Sign

A minus on Econ 102 (macroeconomics) which is decent I suppose, but I basically bombed the final :(

Mahi

A minus is very good. Just find out what happened in the final, as long as you know what happened and do not repeat—it is fine.

Love,
Proud Mummy

A in all my classes, as per usual. Including senior essay! And with so little effort :P So I graduate with a 3.93 and a summa cum laude!

Mahi

Yay, so I am now officially a Mumma cum laude!

Love,
Proud Mummy

A in intro to environmental analysis!
Ashima

Never been happier—with my MahimA and AshimA!!
Mummy

Hi girls

I think you both need to read this, even if you know what it's about, because it is really important as you decide 'what next' after your first degree.

1. Why work?

After an appropriate education is completed, everyone must live off their income, not off their capital (that is, 'sustainability') and a job (in whatever field they choose) is the way to achieve that. Living off capital is unsustainable.

Another way to live off income (and not capital), is to become a skilled investment manager, that is, to earn income from invested capital—but that's a highly specialised job and it takes decades of experience to do it well.

2. What is an 'appropriate education'?

An appropriate education for ALL jobs in ANY business (from selling clothes at a retail store to making loans at a bank), includes acquiring basic skills such as correct spelling, correct grammar in English and one other language, basic mental arithmetic (addition, subtraction, multiplication, division)—this is what your primary and secondary school education in English and maths is supposed to have done, although mental maths was lacking, a lacuna which I am happy to correct, if you allow me to. Appropriate education for any business also includes a basic understanding of economics, which describes the world of business at an aggregated level (that is, macroeconomics) and at an operational level (that is, microeconomics). This is what your A-level in economics is meant to have done, and that's why it was important. In addition, business requires a positive outlook towards the world of business and towards the people you will interact with—that is, you have to want to serve customers, work with colleagues, be able to interact with people, until eventually you can run a business, which consists of making profits by offering whatever the business makes or does to its customers.

In the case of jobs with a high knowledge content (which are not normally 'business' jobs), the 'appropriate education' will also include a degree in that field, to ensure that concepts are familiar. In other words, you cannot lecture on political sciences without studying political sciences, just as you cannot do astrophysics research without a physics degree. Sometimes, an 'appropriate education' can be 'self-education' (for example, do one's own reading and research).

3. Why accept grunt work?

Everyone begins their work life with jobs in any field by doing tasks which may be mundane, or mechanical, or repetitive, but the application of mind and ingenuity to make them more efficient, more effective, less prone to error, or less mundane is the way to impress your employers, and to qualify yourself to be given tasks that are more intellectually challenging, less mundane, more responsible and so on to the next level. Progress from one job to the next in the same domain is called a 'career'. Most people have one career in life, some have two careers (like me), and I even know one or two who are on their third career, but for each switch, they need 'appropriate education'.

All the best and love,

Pops

—Email exchanges between us and the girls while they were at college in 2006–12

▸•◂

As the email exchanges between the girls and us show, academics and careers were often discussed, debated, wept over and celebrated in our family. I did it in the archetypal Indian way, urging the children to do their best, to never be satisfied with an A minus, to always go for an A plus. My urgings were shrill, flouted all rules of balanced parenting and I would not recommend them to everybody. My friends often said jokingly that I had brought up children in such a way that they felt loved only when they got good grades and that my love fluctuated with their grades. That was not the whole truth, but yes, we did celebrate good grades through school and university with extravagant family outings and holidays and the girls always knew that Mummy was 'happy'. I think I managed to infuse pride and joy in academic achievement, which the children grew to share and enjoy despite the sacrifices it sometimes entailed. Even my husband who was very Western and balanced in his approach to most things was accepting of 'grunt work'. So he was Indian in this way—work hard, achieve good academic results and build a career.

Looking back, I started the children on this long journey almost as soon as they were born. Puzzles and games that challenged the mind were bought in preference to dolls and names of dinosaurs were taught with patience and care. I used to sit for hours with them fitting in minute bits of jigsaw puzzles and rejoice when the picture was complete. I delighted in the fact that the children could spell Tyrannosaurus Rex and knew all the various theories about the extinction of dinosaurs. I remember Mahima asking me to buy a penguin soft toy on a holiday to Australia. 'You already have a penguin,' I replied, thinking we had too many soft toys—I was not in favour of soft toys because in my boxed mind they did not encourage any learning at all. 'Mummy, what we have is a Fairy Penguin, this one's an Emperor Penguin,' Mahima shot back in protest.

I was thrilled! A child who knew her penguins deserved to have more than one of them!

I don't know what might have happened, had I encouraged tennis or swimming with equal enthusiasm. Mahima was good at running and managed to win races in her playgroup and early school days. But that did not lead me to enrol her in an athletics programme. That was the Indian parent in me. I myself had little experience of sport and my own parenting had been about studying and excelling. When we returned to India for a few years in their early school years, my own attitude was reinforced by the school. It was a very good school academically, but being in the crowded downtown area of Mumbai, had very limited sports facilities. Whatever the reason, the girls soon took to excelling academically and presenting me with reports that were full of As and excellent remarks by the teachers. There is an interesting story here that I have to break away to tell.

When she was about seven years old, Mahima used to play a game with me whenever she returned with her school report. She would pretend to be very disheartened, say she had got a C overall and I would feign shock and horror. Then she would present her report and it would be As all the way, making us both squeal with delight. Ashima watched all this interestedly and the first time she got a report from school, she came back waving it and beaming all the way. 'I've got all As, Mummy!' she shrieked as she handed me the report card. I said a quick prayer, thanking God that both my clever children were now on their way to the pinnacles of achievement and opened it. To my utter disbelief, there were letters of the alphabet that I had never seen before. Bs and yes, even Cs!

I did not know how to react. Ashima stood by expectantly, waiting for me to squeal and giggle, which according to her was the delightful final act of the 'game'. I realised my little one was focusing on surprise, rather than grades that were the point of our little game. She had done her bit, pretended she had got a grade she hadn't actually got, just like her sister did, and could not understand why Mummy wasn't laughing. I cannot remember what I actually said to my innocent five-year-old, but I think she understood at the end of our little talk that the game had to end only one way—with an A. And after that talk, she did not disappoint!

My pride and joy in my children's academic achievements was the butt of many family jokes. As the girls grew up, they regarded the obsession with academics as one of their mother's strange quirks. I would recount stories of my own academic career, tell them they came from a line of brilliant women and even their grandmother (my mother) had been a rank-holder at Delhi University. Their favourite one was how I got the highest marks in Marathi at school—despite not being a native speaker. Ashima would often joke about my limited knowledge of the English alphabet. 'Mum, there are lots of interesting alphabets out there whom you must meet and get to know,' she would say, 'like B and C and, of course, the interesting D, E and F. Why do you always get stuck with A?'

This obsession with academics did not stop with my own children. I had favourites amongst my friends' children who had 'topped' or 'maxed' something or the other. When we met a lady at a wedding recently and I was trying to explain who she was, one of the girls said brightly, 'Of course we know! Didn't her son get 1550 in his SAT exam and cry, and then sat again and got 1600?' She was right! I had quite forgotten the story but they had remembered the parable of 'never be satisfied with anything but the best' as typified by my friend's geeky son.

The girls also laughed at the way I recounted their academic achievements to total strangers. I once told an absolutely random minicab driver on the way to the airport that my daughter had been accepted for a place at Cambridge University! My explanation that we had passed by a pub called 'Oxford & Cambridge' did not make the story acceptable to two embarrassed girls cringing in the back seat of the cab. Nor the fact that the driver was of Indian origin, empathised with me and congratulated us heartily!

Strangely obsessive as I am, I am pretty sure I am not alone—academic success is integral to the NRI story. In a large number of cases, it is academic brilliance that has brought the parents out of India in the first place and it is natural that they see it as a passport to success. There are thousands of brilliant parents who battled the numerical odds of getting into the Maulana Azad Medical College in Delhi or an Indian Institute of Technology to get to the US or the UK. According to a report by the Indian American Centre for Political Awareness, about 64 per cent of Indian Americans have attained a Bachelor's degree or more, compared to 28 per cent nationally and 44 per cent average for all Asian-American groups. Almost 40 per cent of Indians have a

Master's, doctorate or other professional degree, which is five times the national US average! Then, of course, there's the positive correlation between education and income. The median household income for US residents born in India is $91,195 against a $50,740 average for the total population. A University of California, Berkeley, study reported that one-third of the engineers in Silicon Valley are of Indian descent, while 7 per cent of valley hi-tech firms are led by Indian CEOs.

While this high educational attainment and financial success is not true of all immigrant Indian groups, NRIs broadly see education as the means to a better future for their children. This is in part an 'Indian' characteristic—an attitude, a work ethic, a belief that hard work brings rewards. It is ingrained in the Indian psyche and transported overseas in its most pure form. But it is also an 'immigrant' quality. To establish themselves in their new country, immigrants have traditionally opted for the safest, most conservative careers that bring financial stability and social prestige. While Indians in India are experiencing the new economy and happily embracing careers in media, in music, in design and in art—NRIs urge their children to get good professional qualifications and pursue traditional careers such as medicine and law. Or well-paid ones such as banking and consultancy.

Are we right or justified in expecting academic success from the next generation? Are we helping our children make the most of the ample opportunities that today's world offers? Are we not restricting our children to replicating our own success and follow us on a well-trodden path? My experience shows that NRI parents have been remarkably unadventurous when it comes to academics and careers. I often wonder where the risk-taking gene went? Surely, to come abroad themselves must have meant a risk-taking ability, a desire to experience the new and a fierce determination to conquer fear of the unknown. Yet it all seems to have evaporated. There is this overwhelming urge to play safe and earn money. The number of Indian bankers' children I know who are slaving away in well-paid banking jobs while hating every minute of it, goes into dozens! Or even worse, they kid themselves that derivatives are divine and that they actually love their 105-hour work week, their boss from hell and not having a meaningful life!

Contrast this with, say, the children of American or English well-heeled people. The children do have the cumulative advantages of privilege and wealth in terms of a good education, but they also realise that their parents will leave behind a sizeable amount of money and property—an advantage which frees them up to travel or work with NGOs and charities and use their education to help others. It is not uncommon for an American boy graduating from Harvard to work for an NGO. He might go to Law School later in life or go on to run a think tank, join the government or even settle down in India or Africa, but there is no unseemly hurry to earn money.

A beautiful English girl I know graduated from Oxford

and now runs a very fine charity, which invites famous poets and writers to teach creative writing at inner city schools. She has written a book on English Romantic poets and has had what I consider a very worthy career after graduating eight years ago. Similarly, an English boy who was with our older daughter at school has lived in Vietnam and Cambodia since he graduated, worked in micro-finance and green energy and looks forward to going back to graduate school. Neither of them has earned bonuses, but they have had rich and fulfilled lives and more importantly, are still growing as people. They have not been swamped by heavy-duty jobs where PowerPoint and Excel are the only skills required and, of course, skills at playing office politics once they are senior enough.

So what is it that impels Indian children and their NRI parents? Why do we cramp their style, especially once we have enough money? I know one banker couple who stymied their son's theatrical ambitions by saying, 'How many Othello roles do you think you are going to get?' Yes, he is Indian and dark-skinned and it will be a while before mainstream theatre in the UK accepts dark-skinned leading men, but who knows? He could have been the one to shatter the stained glass ceiling! Think of what the world would have missed out on if M. Night Shyamalan's NRI parents had urged him to become a doctor instead (they are both doctors in the US apparently, and according to Wikipedia, his father wanted him to practise medicine). The fact that he is an acclaimed director today and has a filmography of acclaimed work, such as *The Sixth Sense*, *The Happening* and *The Village* is due in some part to his mother who overruled his father and encouraged her son to follow his dream.

Most NRI mothers, however, display little imagination when it comes to their children's academic careers. Even when confronted with a strong desire on the part of a child to pursue a non-traditional career, there is a small bow to Western-style parenting, followed by a reversion to type. Let me amplify. I have often heard NRI mums discuss their children's non-academic interests with a bemused nonchalance. 'Ishaan is so interested in drums these days, but it will soon pass.' Or 'Gopika wants to do theatre full-time...hopefully, better sense will prevail before she actually has to make choices.' Poor Ishaan and Gopika! They do not have measles that will soon pass or a madness that will be cured with the right therapy. They need to be encouraged to pursue whatever interests them and they may make a successful career in music or theatre. They may not be cut out to excel at academics or do the 'Indian package' at High School, which consists of maths, advanced maths and further maths, but will the parent listen? No.

There are some parents who do relent temporarily. I know a mother who let her son take a gap year to 'get music out of his system'. 'What a good idea,' her sympathetic friends said, 'he will not be able to turn around and say you did not give him a chance.' 'Exactly,

I want him to realise that he has the freedom to do exactly what he pleases and then hopefully, he will come round to doing medicine.' She did not see the irony of her remark, nor the fact that her intelligent son might realise that he was given a token year off in his expected unending quest for academic excellence.

Hopefully, with time and more security in their adopted country, more Indian parents will encourage rather than 'let' or 'allow' their children to pursue whatever they choose to do. Let us be 'Indian' in urging our children to work hard and excel in whatever they do, rather than being 'Indian' in influencing our children's choice of academic subjects and careers.

SUMMARY

Academic success and a strong work ethic are integral to the NRI story. Hence it is not surprising that our children are encouraged to excel academically.

However, most NRIs, often successful themselves, encourage only conservative career choices like medicine and law. This is not necessary.

Take the cue from Indian children in India—they are opting for what interests them, which could range from films and music to design and development work.

Encourage your child to follow his or her passion and interest and work hard at it, even if it is an unconventional choice. That is the secret of success.

8

WHY INDIANS ARE RELUCTANT TO WELCOME FOREIGNERS INTO THE FAMILY

Pardesiyon Se Na Ankhiyan Milana...

Dearest Mama,

Hope you're well. Sorry I haven't called the last couple of days—been very busy attending Savita's son's wedding to an English girl called Elsie. Definitely the wedding of the season. There was the shehnai playing outside the church (she specially flew the troupe over from India) and it was lovely to hear it played live; I don't think I have heard it since my own wedding. In fact, it was very tastefully done, with a beautiful mix of India and the West. They had a church wedding first in Western attire; Savita's son looked like a swarthy Heathcliff in a top hat and tails! The ceremony was very solemn, but beautiful. The bride's father spoke about India being a great civilisation and the bridal couple had chosen a piece from Rabindranath Tagore's Gitanjali as a reading.

Then we drove to a nearby country hotel and the bridal couple had a quick change of costume. Close family members changed too. From hats and floral summer frocks to sarees and turbans. Even the girl's family, her parents and brother and sister slipped into Indian clothes. Savita had taken the trouble to get clothes from India, these were not the gaudy rags that pass for Indian clothes in Bangladeshi or Kenyan-Gujju ghettos here; they were Indian designer clothes—specially commissioned and hand-embellished. Manish Malhotra, someone whispered to me, but I am not sure. He is a famous Bollywood designer so they must have cost the earth.

At the hotel, they had rigged up a beautiful pandal with flower-bedecked poles. They couldn't have a wood fire for health and safety reasons so they had an electronic gas fire specially installed, which looked quite realistic with flames dancing upwards like the one Sanjay has in his Boston home, except his is set in the wall and enclosed by a fake chimney and this was right in the centre. The priest then performed a short ceremony and the bride and the groom read out their vows in English. The Indian section, who had been forced to be quiet in the church, chattered away through the ceremony, shocking all the girl's relatives who sat earnestly in the front rows trying to listen to what the Hindu rituals meant. We happened to be sitting close to the pandal so

I managed to catch the vows. They sounded so strange and alien in English! I was also struck by the importance given to the pursuit of wealth. A Hindu marriage is less about supporting each other through riches or poverty, and more about pursuing prosperity together! At one stage Rohan promised Elsie he would 'not transgress her wishes in earning wealth and fulfilling desires,' and Elsie promised she would 'look after Rohan's material possessions, including his cattle and livestock!'

Later, in the beautiful setting of an English garden and enjoying the dying warmth of the late setting sun, we were served refreshing lychee martinis, mango bellinis and, of course, loads of champagne. There was a buffet dinner served in a marquee. Savita had taken so much trouble over the amazing fusion food—moilee cappuccino which was a kind of frothy soup made out of Kerala coconut gravy and gajar halwa tarts which made me wonder why hadn't someone thought of this earlier? Gajar halwa gets too sweet in large quantities, but this was just right, the bite-sized portions set off by buttery pastry!

—An email to my mother describing an
English–Indian wedding I attended in 2009

Savita seems to have spent a lot of money and being Bengali, she has good taste. We have attended Punjabi NRI weddings here, which are a fusion of the worst of both worlds! Mrs Kapoor's grandson got married to an American girl recently and he insisted on arriving on an elephant! And the food at the wedding was called

Tastes of India, with counters dedicated to India's north, south, east and west. I had ker sengri from the north, chicken chettinad from the south, cholar dal from the east and Goan fish curry from the west. Nothing went with anything else and it was such a colossal waste! I hope Savita's son's marriage lasts. These days divorces are so commonplace and who is to say how foreigners will behave. No point funding these lavish weddings.

—Excerpt from my mother's terse reply

▸•◂

Nowhere does the Us vs Them dilemma come out more than in the *shaadi* stakes. It's natural that who the children marry is important to any parent because their children's long-term happiness depends on it. However, Western-style parenting dictates very firmly that once the children are adults, they are allowed to take their own decisions about their life partner. These decisions may sometimes be wrong, but it would be rare to find a Western mother who would be devastated by her son's choice of wife. At most, it would elicit a sigh and 'as long as she makes him happy, I guess,' from the disappointed mother.

This is not so with many NRI parents. While they may adopt Western norms in terms of lifestyle, clothes and holidays, the *shaadi* territory remains firmly rooted in another land and in another time. While Indians in India (especially in the metros) may have moved on in terms of accepting people from other communities and castes, we still find Tam Brahms (Tamil Brahmins) in the US being rigid about caste as an important matrimonial requirement. Is it about being out of touch with a rapidly modernising India? Is it imagining India to be what it was thirty years ago when they left? Or is it a fear of their identity being swamped by an alien culture? All of the above, I think.

For Indians, whether they live in India or abroad, marriages are not remotely arranged in heaven, but are rather, the result of meticulous planning and plotting by relatives, friends and various well-wishers who bring together 'eligible' boys and girls. A 'good' match is a social triumph in the NRI community just as it is in India. What lends urgency to the NRI effort and an edge to its collective anxiety is the fact that while an unsuitable match in India would still be an Indian person albeit of a different community or caste, outside India, a 'bad' match could mean a foreigner—even worse, a foreigner from a lower social class! In an alien land where social distinctions are blurred, Indian parents find themselves confronting some unexpected dilemmas that they solve in their own unique way. 'Our foreign *bahu*'s father was a partner in an American law firm,' boasts one, 'Our foreign son-in-law went to Cambridge,' informs another. Somehow, introducing social ranking pegs that Indians recognise and respect gives a socially acceptable face to a dubious alliance with a foreign family.

NRI children are often confused about the fact that marriage with an Indian person (particularly from the same community) does not require any validation whatsoever. It is enough to say 'my niece got engaged to the Pathak boy' and everyone knows it's a great match because everyone in the small community that we are addressing in this case, knows that the Pathaks have an ICS lineage, an ancestral house in a posh part of town and the younger set have cushy jobs abroad. Since they have not grown up in India, my children do not know how to peg everyone they meet into the fine web of social hierarchy woven by previous generations. This is not necessarily a bad thing and makes them much more open-minded than people like me. Mahima and Ashima are constantly amazed at my ability to recognise Indian surnames and slot them into regional communities. So a Khanna is from Punjab and a Purandare is from Maharashtra while a Joshi could be a UPite or a Maharashtrian or a Gujarati (but always a Brahmin). However, it is this ability that makes me slot people into preconceived categories and that is surely, not such a good thing.

It is this prejudiced attitude amongst NRI parents that leads to unhappy situations. I know of parents who have steadfastly refused to accept their children's choices or accepted them grudgingly. Marrying an Indian from another community still raises eyebrows amongst some sections of the NRI community. Isn't it time we got over these narrow-minded prejudices and took the lead from our NRI children?

Of course, the objection to marrying non-Indians takes us to a whole new level. We attended a wedding reception recently where it was revealed that the young couple had got married secretly five years ago, but the girl's parents had refused to accept the white British delivery boy their lawyer daughter had chosen as her life partner! It took them five whole years to unveil their dark (or should I say white) secret!

With Indian parents living abroad, the 'danger' that their children will marry someone of their adoptive country is very real. It comes out in all manner of real and imagined fears. 'No BMW,' I cautioned my son, said a lady I met at a lunch, while the others giggled. No Black, Muslim or White (BMW) matches permitted seems to be an old aphorism that loops in both the inherent racism and car obsession of the NRI community so neatly, it deserves a special mention in the long list of visceral reactions to the subject of *shaadi* with foreigners. There are others too. White *bahu*s call you by your name (*sharam hi nahi hai*); foreign sons-in-law cannot put up with in-laws staying in the house for weeks at a time (what does he expect us to do, check into a hotel?); guess what jewellery my daughter got from her German in-laws (a silver bracelet, *hai hai*); Mrs Kapoor's *angrez bahu* put her up in the guest room on the third floor (*uff*...what of her arthritic knees!). The litany of complaints is endless but if you examine these issues, they are relatively minor cultural differences that can easily be bridged with some understanding on both sides. So why does the whole *shaadi* debate stir emotions and bring up such strong reactions?

My hunch is that it is an identity question in its most raw form. It is about genes and race and 'immersing' yourself in the more dominant culture of the host country as opposed to holding your head above the water defiantly. Think of the host country as a vast ocean absorbing all manner of different races. Then think of the first-generation immigrant Indian, swimming furiously to stay afloat, often against the tide. Finally, imagine him watching his dearly beloved son go under without a fight—to disappear and become one with the vast blue. Scary? Definitely.

Does the reaction to children marrying a foreigner vary with the socio-economic status and education in the NRI community? Broadly speaking, it does. In the UK, for instance, at one end of the scale you get immigrant communities firmly rooted in the *pind* or village from where they migrated. They have children who were born and brought up entirely in a foreign land, sound foreign themselves, think like their white British friends and yet have to conform to their parents' outdated views when it comes to marriage. This is the nightmare scenario that leads to honour killings, forced marriages and the racial stereotyping of Indians as backward. In the less extreme and more common cases, it leads to NRIs looking for matches within their own and restricted circles. I remember telling a close friend, who is British Indian, that by looking only for other British Indian men, she was restricting herself to only about 2 per cent of the country's population. What about the other 98 per cent? She looked at me as if I had said something heretical. Years of being single later, she decided to broaden her dating forays and went from 'young Punjabi professionals' (I promise you, they exist!) to mainstream dating agencies and found a white British guy whom she calls her husband today.

Then there are those elite NRIs for whom white is right. Ballet lessons, riding in Hyde Park, French rather than Hindi as a foreign language, expensive private schools—their children have been through it all. Little wonder they think of themselves as global citizens. Their marriages to foreigners (often of the same class) are greeted with squeals of delight by parents who say, 'Sarah is such a de-light-ful girl,' with their well-bred stress on 'light' showing just how far they have come from their Indian accents and roots. So how do these people fit into the vast ocean analogy? With material success, these people have learnt to ride the waves in the sea and their children marrying 'out' are acquiring a surfboard to help ride the waves even better. They do not fear immersion, they are the elite and they will always be above water, so to speak.

The vast majority of NRIs, however, remain ambivalent about the subject of marriage to foreigners. I have a friend who always talked of giving unconditional love to children so long as her son had a foreign girlfriend. The day he proposed to her, she brought up so many conditions, it made her lawyer son's head spin!

The reaction seems to depend entirely on the circumstances of each case and there is a definite preference and hierarchy even amongst the vast pool of foreign spouses. For instance, Europeans are preferred to the Americans and the British because they are more 'family-minded' (whatever that means). Children from stable homes are preferred for obvious reasons. 'Okay, so our daughter-in-law is American, but her parents have had a solid marriage for twenty-seven years.' East Asians are liked for the obvious reason that, 'They have Asian culture in common with us.' Myths have reinforced this complex hierarchical structure of spouse preference, but it does provide mobility and there is much jostling going on to get onto the next higher rung. So, heaven forbid, should your daughter marry a black person, you can actually transcend that by claiming he is related to the former American President!

Having established that marriage is of pressing concern to most NRIs and they continue to see it through the Indian lens of a social contract rather than the joyful union of a couple, what are the means adopted to ensure that NRI children are gently steered in the direction of matrimony? Especially in a world where it is rapidly becoming old-fashioned and irrelevant.

While the traditional meeting-in-the-drawing-room kind of arranged marriages are dying or dead, the 'encouraged' or 'introduced' marriage is thriving. NRI parents realise that their offspring live in a universe of 'foreign' people and their fears that one of these foreigners might slip into their gene pool makes the interest in 'encouraged' matrimony even more keen.

They also realise that their Westernised offspring may

not want to say yes or no after a casual viewing, so dating with an eye on marriage is encouraged. I have heard many Indian parents with children of marriageable age pronounce Western dating websites as an Indian concept. 'What do these websites do if not match up boys and girls according to age, looks and educational background? We Indians have been doing this for generations through arranged marriages!'

This sort of talk encourages their children to agree to introductions within the Indian community and why not? Every trick in the book must be employed to keep them within the Indian family. However, the chance of an 'arranged' introduction succeeding, that is, leading to marriage, is much higher if Indian parents walk the talk. If they claim that they invented dating, then dating rules must be followed. There must be no pressure to marry—let the young boy and girl spend as much time as they need with the other person and give them the assurance that they can walk away without any repercussions.

The Jewish community is widely held up as an example of how genes and wealth can be kept within the community. I have heard Indian parents talk wistfully of how well the Jews have managed to preserve their heritage and traditions. Some go a step further and organise Jewish-style 'minglers' for their single kids. One innovative Indian hostess came up with the idea of a BYOB party with a difference. The BYOB in this case was Bring Your Own *Bachcha*s! Needless to say, it was a big success. Conversation around it was carefully couched in general networking terminology. 'We brought our children because we want them to have really good Indian friends, just as we have had through the years,' said one mother who had specially flown back from a brief holiday in the US to attend the occasion. What she did not say was that she wanted her daughter to pick a spouse from a select group of well-placed NRI boys whom she had known since they were kids.

Sometimes these introductions work. I know of at least three friends whose children married a 'Suitable Indian'. I have known of many others whose children have not obliged and are still single or married to non-Indians. Again, some of these marriages are successful and some are not. So clearly, there is no simple solution.

However, there are some guidelines on how the dating/marriage subject can be approached with good sense. Firstly, do not be afraid to discuss the issue at the family dinner table—I cannot tell you how many young NRIs (especially boys) have been surprised at the depth of feeling their choice of a non-Indian girl has evoked in their parents. 'I had no idea; they always seemed so modern—I mean, Amy had been home and my mother was completely comfortable with her and even Amy said she was amazed my mum spoke such good English.' What this confused young man did not realise was that his mother was hoping that Amy would be a passing fancy!

Stating your preferences in a non-prejudiced, non-partisan way helps. Instead of saying all foreigners are bad (certainly untrue!), it would be better and more acceptable to children if we said, 'We would like nothing more than a considerate and loving partner for you, so make sure you choose carefully.' Stress the values that are required to make a good marriage and you have the best chance of success with your young adult child.

Remember, our NRI children are brought up with the best possible liberal education and they have been taught not to judge on the basis of race. Therefore, the chances of the message getting through is much better if it is non-partisan.

And finally, if your children do pick a non-Indian partner, it is not the end of the world. There are foreign spouses who respect and cherish Indian culture and values. I am sure we all have a foreign aunt from an earlier generation who spent her whole life in India and learnt the local language, cooked Indian food and wore sarees. In London, the person whose opinion I respect on all matters that relate to Indian culture is the English husband of a friend, an Indian. A classical musician and an eminent academician, he plays the piano and the tabla. He has learnt Sanskrit and speaks Hindi and Marathi fluently. He never misses an Indian concert or book reading. My friend says he is more Indian than she is and she is absolutely right! It may also be worth remembering that India as a country, has always welcomed foreigners. If you are north Indian, you were originally, many centuries ago, from foreign stock. Show your new son-in-law or daughter-in-law some true Indian warmth and it will be returned in full measure!

Love and respect are not the preserve of Indians; these are truly international feelings.

SUMMARY

A good match is a social triumph amongst NRI parents, as it is in India. Sometimes more so, because the possibilities of meeting a suitable Indian boy or girl are limited and have to be engineered.

Old-fashioned and prejudiced attitudes such as forbidding the children from dating foreigners or hiding the fact that the child has married against the wishes of the parents do not do us any favours—as Indians or human beings.

Discussing the subject in a non-partisan way, such as emphasising the importance of a loving and considerate partner, is more likely to be heard by your children.

Bring up the subject well before the children start dating, emphasise the importance most Indians place on marriage, how Indians see the marriage as a relationship with the whole family, not just an individual, explain that it is easier for a relationship to succeed if there are things in common with the person one marries, which is why an Indian person may be a better bet.

Use websites and the internet to help your children find suitable matches. Thanks to modern technology, you can have access to a large database of people in the same situation as you. But remember, your children will only accept these encouraged or introduced matches if they are given time and space to make a considered decision.

And finally, if your child does marry a foreigner—show them both some true Indian love and warmth. It is likely to be appreciated and reciprocated.

9

RACISM AND HOW TO DEAL WITH IT

Hum Kaale Hain To Kya Hua... Dilwale Hain!

My belief in an ideal world that respects diversity was put to the test by a high-profile UK media issue a few years ago. It was the racial harassment faced by Bollywood actress Shilpa Shetty on a reality TV show called Celebrity Big Brother. *The format of the show was designed to put diverse and often mutually incompatible personalities under one roof for several weeks and record their every move. The contestants on the show voted for two 'unpopular' housemates and the audience finally got to decide which one was evicted. The winner was finally decided through a weekly process of elimination. Now, normally, watching* Big Brother *can be as boring as watching paint dry and I was not a big fan. I had heard that for the first time, an attractive Indian actress had been roped in to be part of the new series, but that had not motivated me enough to endure unending footage of people brushing their teeth and tossing in their sleep.*

Then suddenly, 'The Race Row' as the tabloids called it, erupted. Apparently, Shilpa Shetty had been bullied and called names by a gang of white girls in the house headed by a British contestant, Jade Goody. For the first time in the series, I, and some three million additional viewers, tuned in. The episode was hurtful and stinging. I was angry and upset when Jade asked Shilpa to 'go back to the slums.' It was humiliation on national television. For the first time in my life, I felt 'Indian' and different. Maybe my dream of being a global citizen was just that—only a dream. It crossed my mind that maybe my British friends saw me as 'Indian' above everything else. Even being a successful and glamorous Bollywood actress was not enough insulation against racist remarks that stripped you down to the colour of your skin and the GDP of your country, and I was just an ordinary person. Maybe London was not the open-minded, cosmopolitan city I had thought of as home. I felt fragile and vulnerable—but not for long. Popular opinion in the UK came out strongly against the offensive bullying. The main sponsor of the show pulled out in protest. And finally, when the audience votes came in, Jade had to leave the house. Shilpa went on to win the show and become a household name in the UK.

Today, some years later, I can look back on the unsavoury episode calmly and think about all the good that came out of it. It forced me to judge Jade's crass remarks against the weight of my beliefs, my values and my entire upbringing. While my first reaction was to be hurt and humiliated, deeper reflection made me realise that she was speaking out of ignorance and prejudice.

At a deeper level, the issue also made me confront my feelings about racism and being Indian. I realised I was very proud of my country of origin and indeed, of my race. Finally, this experience helped strengthen my belief in diversity rather than shatter it. By embracing diversity, we all become better global citizens. I realise I have been particularly fortunate: my diverse background has given me both the courage and the vision to have a broader worldview than most people and made me more accepting of differences amongst people—and race is just one of those differences that ought to be celebrated.

—Ashima writing on the Shilpa Shetty race row

We do not like to think about it. We certainly do not talk about it. Some of us do not even acknowledge it. Yet racism exists and is a part of life for Indians living in many countries outside India. We have all walked past youths yelling 'Pakis' and ignored them, hurrying along just that extra bit of distance to get out of earshot; we have learnt to bury our heads in the sand or even brought ourselves to laugh about some of the epithets hurled at us—'*Chinki Chink and Bindi Bind*' was a creative one thrown at a Chinese-Indian pair of girlfriends! We tell ourselves that racists are ignorant and illiterate and have no place in a rapidly globalising world. That racism is doomed and will surely die out as the internet and transport links bridge barriers between people.

But will it happen before our children grow up? Before they learn to detect that slight impropriety in tone which may or may not be racial? Before they learn that hurt and humiliation has been the lot of many economically deprived Indians who have struggled as immigrants in their early years? It used to be said by rich Indians travelling abroad that they hated getting off at Heathrow airport in London because invariably, the toilet attendants were Indian ladies from Southall. Well, that has changed. In the UK, second-generation immigrants have done extremely well and now run successful businesses and hold jobs in law firms and banks; but talk to them and you can see the chip on the shoulder remains. Their parents' hurt and humiliation in the early days (often felt, never said) makes them want to succeed that much more. In British-Indian families, the wounds of racism run deep. There is a moving scene in Gurinder Chadha's film *Bend it like Beckham*, where Anupam Kher playing an Indian immigrant father, owns up to his hurt and humiliation at being kept out of a racist English cricket team after thirty years and lets his daughter do the unthinkable—play football and have a white boyfriend.

Unfortunately, despite increasing globalisation and the rise of India as an economic powerhouse, racism is alive and well. It exists, despite us pushing it under the carpet and never mentioning it, let alone discussing it with our children. Yes, we talk about it when Shah Rukh Khan gets held up at JFK airport for several hours while they search his luggage but then, 'his name is Khan', the Hindus amongst us tell ourselves. I think it is time we stopped kidding ourselves. Hindu or Muslim, Shah Rukh is an Indian icon. So the first step in dealing with racism is to acknowledge it.

The second step is to realise that we Indians are 'racist' ourselves when it comes to others. From stereotyping all white people as parent-haters and all blonde girls as 'fast'—we have a long way to go as a non-partisan community that can object to racism. We are quick to anger when it happens to us but totally lacking self-awareness about our own shortcomings. So as parents, the first step is to dismantle our own prejudices and teach the children to respect all human beings. The children are quick learners and given the unbiased environment around them, can end up teaching their parents a thing or two!

Racism is easy to recognise and deal with when it comes in a nasty overt form. The racial abuse hurled at Asians in the UK, the rude shopkeeper in Hong Kong who tells you to stop wasting his time, the Singaporean Chinese friend who tells you that before she met you she thought all Indians were dirty and smelly, the posh shop assistant at a Paris boutique who refused to attend to you, or the waiter in the Michelin-starred restaurant who keeps avoiding eye contact. These could all be instances which you decide to ignore as one-offs. If they have happened with your children around, they will notice them but not know how to deal with them. The answer in these cases is to be firm but polite. Do NOT ever lose your temper. That will only conform to their racist image of Indians being an impolite and uncivilised lot. Always occupy the moral high ground. Be more civilised and polite than the person who is treating you badly. Shame them into submission—it always works. Your children will learn to deal with racial prejudices in the same way. Politeness, with a bit of humour, will give them a feeling of superiority at the end of the encounter. Gandhi was a master of the racial put-down. Asked what he thought of Western civilisation, he answered, 'I think it will be very good idea'...centuries of colonisation and racial inferiority wiped out with one witty remark!

A friend of mine, a doctor, recounted an apocryphal story in this regard. She was shopping at a large department store in London with her daughter and holding up a dress against her daughter to see how it looked. Just then a small white lady came by and mistook her for a shop assistant, 'Would you know where the coats are?' she asked innocently. My friend was unfazed. This was her one afternoon off in her busy week, valuable time with her daughter and she did not want to get upset. 'I wish I knew,' she replied with a merry tinkling laugh, 'but the only coat I ever seem to get into is my white coat; I am a doctor, you see.' The small white lady scurried off after a weak smile. And I am sure my friend's daughter was proud that her mother dealt with the situation in a good-humoured, but capable way. Just like a good doctor!

Racism in a covert form, on the other hand, is much more difficult to identify and deal with. It can occur in the workplace or when you are trying to find an apartment to rent. It is never an open and direct insult, hence difficult to counter. The refusal to promote you could be couched in all sorts of professional excuses. The glass ceiling for Indians in the corporate world could be just that—a glass ceiling—and you wouldn't know it exists until you bump your head against it. The difficulty in finding a job could be papered over by potential employers as a lack of appropriate qualifications or a particular language requirement. In Singapore, for instance, a lot of Indians feel shut out of the job market because job advertisements want Mandarin-speakers.

In 2009, a government sting operation reported by the *Guardian* newspaper in the UK uncovered widespread racial discrimination against workers with African or Asian names. Researchers sent 3,000 applications under false identities and found that the same CV, when it went under an Asian or African name needed to be sent to sixteen employers before it got an interview whereas those with an English-sounding name got an interview or encouraging phone call with just nine tries.

There is no easy answer here, except to prepare your children. Tell your children racist discrimination in the job market does not necessarily happen and should not happen, but also tell them they just have to try harder. It is part of the territory of being a minority, of being an immigrant, of being a foreigner. Positive reinforcement helps. There are any number of corporate success stories, of Indian achievements internationally that will drive the point home. From Sabeer Bhatia, the founder of Hotmail to Amar Bose, the inventor of the Bose sound system, there have been Indians who have achieved their dreams and they have been the same colour as you and me. From Indira Nooyi (Pepsi) to Anshu Jain (Deutsche Bank), Satya Nadella (Microsoft), Sundar Pichai (Google) and Rakesh Kapoor (Reckitt Benckiser), there have been Indians who have scaled the corporate ladder right to the top in American and European companies. Your children can do it too. And some good old-fashioned Indian hard work will do no harm!

As parents, we might think it is our duty to instil only the best in our children and it is easy to paint a picture of an ideal world where cultural and racial differences amongst people are celebrated and enjoyed. Indian children growing up outside India often attend international schools or highly cosmopolitan schools in large ethnically diverse cities. In London, for instance, they could easily be living in an apartment block with French neighbours, have Lebanese food available down the road and find a Malaysian best friend. In fact, the school my children attended in Singapore, the United World College of Southeast Asia, prides itself on building global citizens. It lists amongst its guiding principles that, 'education should take place within a diverse college community. The selection of students should ensure representation from regions and social groups that reflect the wide range of tensions among and between people.'

As any parent will tell you, the UWCSEA practises what it preaches. I remember one United Nations evening (yes, they celebrate that), when Ashima first played the gongs in an Indonesian gamelan ensemble dressed in a *batik*-print sarong, then rushed backstage to change into a red-checked knee-length robe to do a Masai dance, finally ending up in her school uniform to sing '*We Are the World*'. I still remember her in that avatar, my nine-year-old believer in diversity, her shining eyes and smiling face reflecting her optimism and belief in an ideal world. Aren't our children entitled to be innocent, even naïve? Must we destroy their idealism with talk of racism every time we read a news report of Indians being attacked? And isn't there a danger that we will raise children with a chip on their shoulder, ready to assume that all slights, all rude behaviour is racist? Or children who cannot understand cultural differences amongst races and assume they have been insulted? I remember a friend's son who had come to study in London remarking that people were so racist. When probed further he said his observation was based on the fact that people in buses do not sit next to him and go and look for empty seats. Now anyone who knows the British will know that it is the British concept of personal space operating here and has nothing to do with race. If he had looked carefully, he would have noticed that they do not sit next to each other either, if they can help it. So clearly, the key to discussing racism with children has to be balance.

No right age can be identified as the time to draw children into a discussion on racism. It depends on circumstances. An Indian family living in Australia for instance, could choose to discuss prejudices and race in the context of news reports that Indians are being attacked. An Indian family in the US could use the attacks on Sikhs in the aftermath of 9/11 as an example of how ignorance and prejudice led to white Americans mistaking turbanned Sikhs for Islamic followers of Osama bin Laden. In Germany, where there is not much of an Indian population, I know an Indian family who never had occasion to discuss racism, until German IT companies raced to recruit Indian software engineers in the late '90s. This led to the infamous right-wing slogan *Kinder nicht Inder* (Children not Indians), which galvanised opinion against Indians. This came as a rude shock to this well-integrated family who had lived in Germany for over twenty years, spoke German fluently and thought only Turkish people (who did the menial jobs) were discriminated against!

In fact, a context always makes the discussion more meaningful and relevant. This could be historical or current. For instance, your children could be studying colonialism at school—this could provide the background against which historical patterns of Indian migration could be discussed at home. In Malaysia and the West Indies, the Indian immigrants were mostly plantation labour and this could account for the prejudice of the locals and their view of Indians as dirty or smelly or poor. In the UK, Indians originally migrated as factory labour for the burgeoning textile industry in the Midlands and obviously, some of that perception of Indians as labourers remains. A friend's husband who worked with an Imperial Chemical Industries plant in Cheshire was often asked 'Which shift?' by people who did not know he held a PhD in chemistry from Oxford University!

Contrast this attitude with the US where the Indian migration pattern has been totally different. Highly skilled engineers, doctors and other professionals have made the US their home and Indians are well regarded and respected. A 2012 report by the Washington-based Pew Research Centre put the household median income of Indian households in the US at $88,000, which is significantly higher than the average US household income of $49,000. This is supported by a high level of education (80 per cent hold college or advanced degrees) and translates into a perception of the community as affluent and educated. The US is also a melting pot in the truest sense and Indians hardly ever feel racially discriminated against.

Apart from historical factors that have shaped attitudes about Indians, there is the current economic scenario. This could also be used to set the stage for discussing a delicate topic in a value-neutral way. In recent years, as Western economies have shrunk and extreme right-wing parties have gained ground in many Western countries, the anti-immigrant feeling has become stronger. In cases where the immigrants are of a different race, they become easier to identify and victimise. Obviously, when the size of the pie gets smaller, the competition gets more fierce. Why should jobs which are so scarce, go to foreigners? Consequently, both the US and the UK have tightened work visa rules. Companies have to justify to their government that they cannot find a local British or American person to fill the job before they can give it to a foreigner. While this can be construed as a form of racism, it is important to understand that this is more about economic scarcity than racism. The right-wing UKIP (United Kingdom Independence Party), for instance, is also against white Europeans who compete for the same jobs and cannot be barred from entering Britain because of European Union rules. The anti-Islam wave triggered by terrorist attacks has not helped. Indians are difficult to tell from Pakistanis and Bangladeshis, who are predominantly Muslim, and this often leads to misplaced suspicion and hate. In fact, there are several factors operating in today's world which could set the stage for a topical discussion of race in your home.

A friend's son had an interesting story to tell about prejudice. During his undergraduate years at the University of Virginia in the US, he was asked to design his own T-shirt for a very special day on campus to celebrate the breakdown of prejudices. He painted the words, 'I am Indian but I am not here to take your job!' on his T-shirt to walk away with applause and the first prize!

In all discussions about racism, it is important not to come across as angry or prejudiced yourself. Children pick up attitudes without your ever having to teach them. And we Indians are unfortunately and notoriously prejudiced. Look at this definition of racism and measure your own beliefs against it. 'Prejudice, discrimination or antagonism directed against someone of a different race based on the belief that one's own race is superior.' Now think back to the times when you have criticised white people for not being family-minded, or blacks for being—well, blacks. So are we Indians racist? Definitely.

In India's colour-conscious, hierarchical society, prejudice is built-in, an automated response to the classification of caste and community. If we as parents have grown up in India, we are conditioned to make distinctions amongst people. Sometimes these assumptions are good. 'He is Bengali so he must be artistic,' or 'She is Tamilian, so she must be clever.' Sometimes they are bad. 'She is so dark and ugly, who will marry her?' In either case, they attribute a set of characteristics to a person based on his community or physical appearance that is very close to the definition of racism. As educated people, we know the fallacy of such assumptions. So why do we fall into these traps of habit again and again? My UWCSEA-schooled children were the first to reprimand me on this. My assumptions about 'foreigners', and just about everyone, were systematically dismantled by my vigilant children, who would point out that I was making an assumption based on prejudice. So the second step in dealing with racism is to make sure you dismantle your own prejudices.

I remember one of Mahima's good friends at her university was a Tanzanian girl who had grown up in Dar-es-Salaam. She came to visit us one spring break and the conversation led to boyfriends and other pre-occupations of the young. 'Why don't you find a nice, tall basketball player?' I asked this tall, beautiful black girl. She sighed and said 'Aunty (Tanzanians use this address too!), I cannot relate to black Americans at all. They seem to have a chip on their shoulder about being black, whereas I have grown up in a black majority country so I have never felt "black", if you know what I mean.' It was the simplest, most effective lesson I ever learnt regarding the fact that the world is not 'black' and 'white'! There are all kinds of people within each sub-group and to pair this Tanzanian girl with a black American based on just her colour and race was wrong. I would never do it again.

So my final point on discussing racism is—learn from your children if you have to! While they may need some guidance and historical perspective on Indian immigration through their early years, your children are likely to grow up as mature, thinking young adults with a healthy respect for all races. They will question and challenge your own beliefs sometimes and hard as it may be, it is time to stop being colourist, communal, or casteist and believe in the world your children want to build.

SUMMARY

Racism should be acknowledged and discussed—not brushed under the carpet. Doing it in a current or historical context puts it in perspective for children.

If you encounter racism while you are with your children, deal with it politely but firmly. This will set the tone for them.

Prepare your children for an unequal world—especially when jobs and resources are scarce. Tell them that they can make up by working hard.

Inspire them with success stories of Indians—there are plenty to choose from.

Finally, dismantle your own prejudices before you educate your children. We Indians are notorious for our own complex hierarchy with its inbuilt 'racism' amongst our own people.

10

THE LAST WORD

Bachpan ke Din Bhi Kya Din The

It is only fitting that the epilogue of this book should be written by the children who were the object of my affections, but also the subject of my lectures all their lives and because I have never said it before (Indian mothers don't—easily) let me say it now and publicly: 'I am very proud of both of you'.

MAHIMA

'Growing up, I saw how little it mattered what I thought of India—the world at large adjudicated on what it meant to be Indian—one minute it meant belonging to a backward country best known for female infanticide, dowries and arranged (read forced) marriages; another, it was the birthplace of a great religion, all-knowing gurus and trending henna tattoos. One minute, it was a place of dire poverty, another, a huge economic opportunity, a market rivalling China's. My own life mirrored this, in a strange Saleem Sinai-esque way. I moved (or was moved) from Mumbai to London, speaking only Hindi and entered into a very English prep-school: I was the only girl in my class with black hair, and I really wanted red, like the Little Mermaid. That was one of my first self-conscious memories.

We then moved back to Mumbai where my British accent was made fun of by my 'Indian' classmates so comfortable in their own skins. I spent those years thinking 'abroad' meant anywhere that was not India, and feeling like we were at the centre of the world. We then moved to Singapore, to an international school, where I initially maintained vestigial Indian classroom habits, like standing up to answer a question. My deferential Indianness was hilarious to my peers and embarrassing for my teachers. Later on, I mastered the art of harnessing Indianness to my advantage—as a teenager, one really wants to be different, and I crawled excitedly into the niche my Indianness had already carved out for me in an international setting. These were the years of crushes on Bollywood stars, hosting cricket World Cup parties, and eventually founding and leading a girl's cricket team, appropriately named 'The No Balls'!

I then moved to London, where I proactively explored my Indian identity. I looked into the past, taking up Kathak and learning about the nuances in Indian culture and religion through classical dance. I looked at the present, and noted the sheer breadth within the modern Indian experience—I was different from my British

Indian friends, just as Arundhati Roy was different from Jhumpa Lahiri. And I took a stand on the future, forming an opinion on Indian politics, both national and global, at a time when the Congress party had just won the elections, and India was vying for a permanent seat on the UN Security Council.

The only constant through all of this pitching back and forth through my global experience of Indianness was my mother's clear and confident insistence that it was, at the end of the day, my foundation. It was the identity I had to build my other identities off, and not something to be discarded at will or lightly draped when it was convenient. My mother fed us on a diet of Indian pride, but beyond that, she put a lot of practical effort into giving us access to the tools, experiences and thinking required to solidify that foundation. After I graduated from university, I put my mother's grooming to the ultimate test, moving (of my own accord, for the first time) to Mumbai to work there for a year. I was happy to find I had a healthy relationship with India and Indianness: I was comfortable as I navigated my way through the crowded streets and haggled with shopkeepers, and I was also emotionally at ease: I didn't have complicated feelings about 'roots' or 'home' or 'foreignness'. I am Indian, and I am many other things on top of that—I don't feel the need to choose. Thank you, Mom, for helping us build that solid foundation!'

Ashima

'I've always loved adopting local culture wherever we moved—throughout my teens, and to some extent my early twenties, I didn't want to stand out or be different. I'd initially hated the turmoil of moving across continents, but as soon as I got to my newest place I'd call home, I immediately turned into a stereotype (pub-going Brit, thanksgiving meal-cooking American). My common thread was always my Indianness. No matter where we were in the world, I felt secure in what Indian culture meant to me, and I understood it well. I used this foundation to be able to pick and choose the best of the additional cultures that surrounded me.

Mom is right when she says it was not easy to get us both to this point. I remember she would always end a long lecture with 'When you grow up, you'll understand why I'm forcing you to do XYZ'. I resented it at the time, but boy, was she right! I am so impressed by the persistence she showed—I was an incredibly difficult child to deal with, especially when it came to Hindi lessons—but I'm unreservedly thankful now.

Knowing an Indian language helps connect with a country, a culture, an economy, as nothing else can. At my workplace, where we're beginning to explore projects in India, I am able to contribute and comment knowledgably and professionally. I relish the surprise when people find out I know how to play the tabla. And at eighteen, being able to guide my English friends through India on holiday, for me, felt like the first truly adult thing I'd done in my life.

If I had to advise other people in the same situation as me, I would say, find the parts of being Indian that mean the most to you and embrace them. For instance, I loved the food but not the ghee, the cricket but not the crowds, the shopping but not the bargaining, Bollywood but not the dancing, the countryside and wildlife but not the cities so much, the hugs from relatives and their unconditional love and warmth but not being forced to eat so much! India is many things. It is different for everybody; but we are fortunate, as being Indian gives us so much to choose from.

I hope I can be as patient and persistent as my mum when it is my turn to teach my children.'

THANK YOU

East or West is the third crowd-curated book co-published by Bloody Good Book and Westland Ltd. Its publication wouldn't have been possible without the contributions of these and many other Bloody Good Bookers. Thank you all for reading and reviewing *East or West* on www.bloodygoodbook.com. Your vote helped us discover this wonderful book!

Sumita Chatterjee
Anshika Alch
Harish Prasad
Geetha Krishnan
Nisha Sinha
Anish Patilkar
Asha Krishna
Resham
Prashant Dutta
Sonu Wig
Rishi Chanda
Ashima
Leela
Vaibhav Kaul
Priyanka Vermani
Maithili Kumar Agarwal
Rashmi Guha
Aditi
Shanta Acharya
Ashish Saxena
Alka Deol
Vishal Grover
Mina Mashru
Surendra Mohanty
Suniti Wali
Alison

Ashima Sukhdev
Sudhanshu M Nayak
Joseph Mariathasan
Christine Menager
Priyanka Sharma
Suman
Gayathri Manikandan
Suman Chhabria Addepalli
Aditi
Marty Lucente
Reiner Zeldenrust
Sarita Chand
Meghana Joshi
Apurv Nagpal
Deepak Kaul
Vijay S
Niyati Shinde
Malu Patel
Anjali Asnanee
Lena Padukone
Kavita Budhraja
Ranjana Sood
Vishal
Anupama
Vijay Ganju
Anandita
Rajen Padukone
Anna Davis
Sheetal
Shaila Mallik
Nimita
Rachna
Tanya Braun
Shivani Kak
Sheila Surya
Pandustar
Saroj Tikku
Nandita
Bhaskar Rao
Dinesh Verma
Maya Kak
Khushal Chand Thakur
Karishma Khullar
Aditya Jayanthi
Meera Kaul
Nalini Kak
Samita Agarwal
Dhruv Khullar
Ritu
Kiran Khullar
Apu Patwardhan
Shailja
Revathi Santhanam
Arati Kaul
Shoto Banerji
Zarine
Priya Tikku
Maya Parmar
Sreerupa
Zahra

Vids
Navpreet Mann
Ranjita Kulkarni
Dhananjaya Chak
Prerna
Abha
Mridu Parmar
Anjana
Mahima
Amit Gupta
Sukh Kak
Naina Knoess
Anna Kortekaas